BR STEAM MOTIVE POWER DEPOTS

DEPOTS

NER

Paul Bolger

Nottingham

Booklaw Publications

First published 1984

© Paul Bolger 1984

This edition published by
Book Law Publications 2009

Printed and Bound by
The Amadeus Press, Cleckheaton, BD19 4TQ.

Preface

The purpose of this book is to assist the average
enthusiast be he modeller, relic collector or historian
with his search for information on motive powe
depots — the home of the steam locomotive.

Many devotees will recall the experience o
touring such an establishment; the hiss of steam, the
clank of engine movements and the sight of smoke
suspended from the ceilings above the many
varieties of engine in different stages of repair.

The sight of a fully serviced locomotive simmering
outside the Depot on a crisp bright morning is a
memory I shall never forget. I hope that the following
pages aid the reminiscences of those fortunate
enough to have lived during the steam age.

This book is dedicated to the many people who
contributed photos and information to this series o
books. A sincere thank you to one and all.

Paul Bolger

The eastern end of Heaton shed in 1954.
Photomatic

Introduction

For reasons of parity with the previous volumes — *BR Steam Motive Power Depots LMR, ER, ScR, SR* and *WR*(all Ian Allan) — the depots covered by this work have been restricted to those which possessed a code, as these were the most visited and of greater importance to the railway network.

In all, 35 depots are outlined and because of the lesser number of sheds by comparison with previous volumes, an average of five views per shed have been included. For continuity of the text the codes used as headings are c1950.

Acknowledgements

This book has been made possible with the invaluable help of the following people and organisations: Mr Winch and Mr Fairclough of Cambridge University Library; Mr G. M. Kichenside of Locomotive & General Railway Photographs; Mr T. J. Edgington of the National Railway Museum; Mr C. J. Woolstenholmes of the North Eastern Railway Association; Miss S. Percy of the Ordnance Survey; Mr C. Turner of Photomatic.

In addition, special thanks are extended to the following: G. Baxter; E. D. Bruton; I. S. Carr; D. Carville; H. C. Casserley; K. Crabtree; A. G. Ellis; K. Fairey; V. Forster; B. K. B. Green; R. A. Griffiths; D. Hardy; T. A. Heyes; B. Hilton; M. S. Houlgrave; P. G. Jump; P. J. Kelley; R. Lidster; B. J. Lynch; F. Lyon; B. Morrison; C. H. S. Owen; J. A. Peden; K. Pike; W. Potter; N. E. Preedy; V. M. Rayne; D. Rendell; E. Scarlett; N. Skinner; J. L. Stevenson; W. T. Stubbs; M. F. Thorley; D. Tyreman; J. Ward; M. S. Welch; and F. Wright.

In the course of preparation the following publications were of major importance as reference and consultative material: *The Railway Observer* (Volumes 18 to 38); *Railway Magazine* (Volumes 94 to 114), *Railway World* (Volumes 19 to 29); *Trains Illustrated* and *Modern Railways* (Volumes 3 to 21).

Notes about Contents

In 1956 and 1957 regional boundary changes resulted in 15 depots, of hitherto LMR and ER control, being transferred to the North Eastern Region. Of these 14 were catered for by the provision of new groups 55 and 56. (For explanatory notes concerning each refer to 55A to 55G and 56A to 56G within the main text.) The other shed, Goole (ex-LMR 25C and of LYR origin) became 53E and later 50D. All 15 depots have been included in the LMR and ER volumes in accordance with their respective origins and initial BR groupings.

Strict compliance with the coding system would have resulted in severe duplication of the contents of this and the afore-mentioned volumes. A balance has, therefore, been struck in an attempt to combat this. It is hoped that the resulting regional 'limbo' where it occurs will not hinder your enjoyment of the book.

Pre-Grouping Origins

Although, primarily, not relevant to the period covered, an indication of the vintage of the shed is given by the inclusion of the company of ownership prior to 1923. This is not necessarily the company which commissioned the building, as many smaller installations were absorbed into the larger companies by the takeover or amalgamation of district railways.

Gazetteer References

These numbers refer to the page and square within the Ian Allan *Pre-Grouping Atlas* which pinpoint the subject's national location.

Closing Dates

The dates given indicate the closure of the depot to steam engines only. However, in some cases the date would have been the same for diesels where the building closed completely, either as a result of its dilapidated condition or the effects of the 'Beeching' cuts.

Shed-Codes

The North Eastern Region was not issued with shed-codes at the outset of nationalisation in 1948 owing to BR's indecision over districts. In 1949 it was allocated ex-LMS type codes in groups 50 to 54. The 55 and 56 sets were added much later — see 'Notes about Contents'.

Allocations

Where the depot's lifetime allows, three separate allocations, of steam locomotives only, are listed from the years 1950, 1959 and 1965. These lists are accurate to August 1950, April 1959 and April 1965.

Plans

All the plans have been based upon the Ordnance Survey County and National Grid series maps from various years and reproduction is by permission of the Controller of Her Majesty's Stationery Office, Crown Copyright Reserved.

Photographs

All except 16 of the 175 illustrations have been restricted to the period 1948/67. The majority of the views are hitherto unpublished and represent many years of search.

50A YORK

Pre-Grouping Origin: NER
Gazetteer Ref: 21 C5
Closed: 1967
Shed-Code: 50A (1949-1967)
Allocations: 1950

Class A1 4-6-2
60121 *Silurian*
60138 *Boswell*
60140 *Balmoral*
60146 *Peregrine*
60153 *Flamboyant*

Class A2 4-6-2
60501 *Cock o' the North*
60502 *Earl Marischal*
60503 *Lord President*
60522 *Straight Deal*
60524 *Herringbone*
60526 *Sugar Palm*

Class V2 2-6-2
60837
60839
60843
60847 *St Peter's School York AD627*

60856	60925	60954	60974	60981
60864	60929	60960	60975	60982
60901	60933	60961	60976	
60904	60934	60962	60977	
60907	60941	60963	60978	
60918	60946	60968	60979	

Class B1 4-6-0
61015 *Duiker*
61016 *Inyala*
61020 *Gemsbok*
61038 *Blacktail*
61071
61084
61115
61239
61288
61337

Class B16 4-6-0

61416	61430	61448	61458	61468
61417	61434	61449	61459	61472
61418	61435	61450	61460	61471
61419	61436	61451	61461	61474
61420	61437	61452	61462	61475
61421	61438	61453	61463	61476
61422	61439	61454	61464	61477
61423	61441	61455	61465	
61424	61443	61456	61466	
61426	61444	61457	61467	

Class D20 4-4-0
62369

Class D49 4-4-0
62726 *The Meynell*
62727 *The Quorn*
62736 *The Bramham Moor*
62740 *The Bedale*
62742 *The Braes of Derwent*
62744 *The Holderness*
62745 *The Hurworth*
62759 *The Craven*
62760 *The Cotswold*
62761 *The Derwent*

Class Q5 0-8-0
63270

Class J21 0-6-0
65043   65075

Class J24 0-6-0
65619

Class J25 0-6-0

65656	65679	65700	65708	65723

Class J27 0-6-0

65845	65861	65885	65890
65849	65883	65888	65894

Looking east to York North in 1952. W. Potter

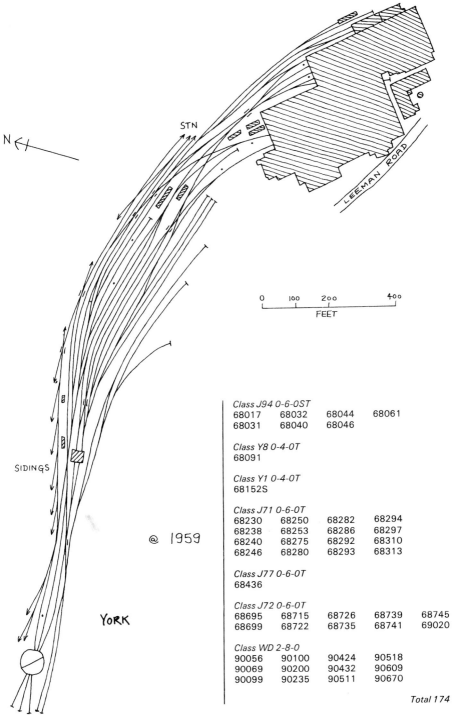

N ←

STN

LEEMAN ROAD

| 0 | 100 | 200 | | 400 |
FEET

SIDINGS

@ 1959

YORK

Class J94 0-6-0ST
68017   68032   68044   68061
68031   68040   68046

Class Y8 0-4-0T
68091

Class Y1 0-4-0T
68152S

Class J71 0-6-0T
68230   68250   68282   68294
68238   68253   68286   68297
68240   68275   68292   68310
68246   68280   68293   68313

Class J77 0-6-0T
68436

Class J72 0-6-0T
68695   68715   68726   68739   68745
68699   68722   68735   68741   69020

Class WD 2-8-0
90056   90100   90424   90518
90069   90200   90432   90609
90099   90235   90511   90670

Total 174

5

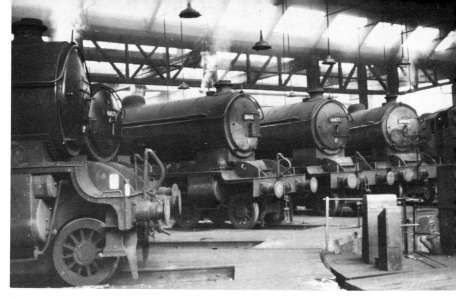

Allocations: 1959

Class 2 2-6-2T
41252

Class 4 2-6-4T
42083   42085

Class 2 2-6-0
46480   46481

Class 3F 0-6-0T

47239	47334	47418	47436	47556
47254	47403	47421	47448	47607

Class A1 4-6-2
60121 *Silurian*
60138 *Boswell*
60140 *Balmoral*
60146 *Peregrine*
60153 *Flamboyant*

Class A2 4-6-2
60501 *Cock o' the North*
60502 *Earl Marischal*
60503 *Lord President*
60512 *Steady Aim*
60515 *Sun Stream*
60522 *Straight Deal*
60524 *Herringbone*
60526 *Sugar Palm*

Class V2 2-6-2
60828
60837
60839
60847 *St Peter's School York AD627*

60855	60878	60925	60960	60975
60856	60887	60939	60961	60977
60864	60895	60941	60963	60981
60876	60907	60946	60968	60982
60877	60918	60954	60974	

Class B1 4-6-0
61002 *Impala*
61053
61069
61071
61084
61086
61288
61337

Class B16 4-6-0

61410	61423	61439	61452	6146
61413	61424	61440	61453	6146
61416	61426	61441	61454	6146
61417	61430	61443	61455	6146
61418	61434	61444	61457	6147
61419	61435	61448	61460	6147
61420	61436	61449	61461	6147
61421	61437	61450	61462	6147
61422	61438	61451	61463	6147

Class K1 2-6-0

62046	62049	62056	62061	6206
62048	62050	62057	62062	

Class D49 4-4-0
62740 *The Bedale*

Class J25 0-6-0
65698   65714

Class J27 0-6-0

65845	65883	65890
65874	65887	65894

6

'A4' 4-6-2 No 60019 Bittern *in store at York North in 1968.* K. Fairey

Class J94 0-6-0ST
68032   68040   68046   68061

Class J71 0-6-0T
68309

Class J77 0-6-0T
68392   68431

Class J72 0-6-0T
68677   68687   68736   69016   69020

Class 3 2-6-0
77012

Class WD 2-8-0
90068   90230   90405   90445   90543
90200   90236   90424   90475   90578

Total 150

Allocations: 1965

Class 4MT 2-6-0
43055   43097   43133
43071   43126   43138

Class A1 4-6-2
60121 *Silurian*
60138 *Boswell*
60145 *Saint Mungo*
60146 *Peregrine*
60152 *Holyrood*
60155 *Borderer*
60156 *Great Central*

Class V2 2-6-2
60810
60828
60831
60837
60847 *St Peter's School York AD627*
60876   60886   60929
60877   60895   60963

'J77' 0-6-0T No 68392 (50A) at rest inside York North in 1959. B. Morrison

7

'B16' 4-6-0 No 61453 (50A) alongside the newly constructed straight shed at York North in 1959.
B. Morrison

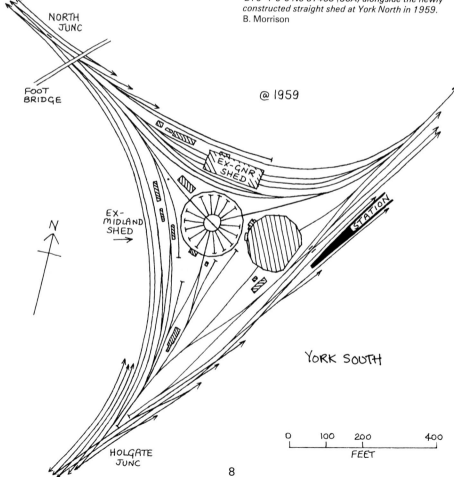

NORTH JUNC

FOOT BRIDGE

@ 1959

EX-GNR SHED

N

EX-MIDLAND SHED

STATION

YORK SOUTH

HOLGATE JUNC

0   100   200   400

FEET

8

The interior of the ex-Midland shed at York South in 1952. N. E. Preedy

Class B1 4-6-0
61002   Impala
61018   Gnu
61021   Reitbok

61049	61256	61276	61319
61176	61275	61303	61337

Class K1 2-6-0

62005	62028	62049	62060
62010	62042	62056	62062
62012	62046	62057	62065

Class J27 0-6-0

65823	65844	65846	65894

Class WD 2-8-0

90045	90078	90217	90517	90518

Class 9F 2-10-0

92005	92205	92211	92231
92006	92206	92221	92239

Total 64

'J72' 0-6-0T No 68722 in early BR livery inside the ex-Midland shed at York South in 1948. It will be seen that the roof was considerably more intact in this year. H. C Casserley

9

York sheds consisted of two main establishments, the quadruple roundhouse at York North (or Clifton as it was sometimes called) and the two separate and singular equivalents at York South. Of the latter, the ex-Midland shed was roofless by 1953 and engines ceased visiting either building in 1961. In 1958 York North was remodelled when two of its roundhouses gave way to a straight road structure.

York North was closed to steam in June 1967 when its last two 'B1' class locos transferred to Low Moor 56F. The depot retained its facilities however as it hosted the occasional visitor via steam 'specials'.

The much renovated building today forms the nucleus of the National Railway Museum.

The remains of both roundhouses at York South in 1963 as viewed from the station platform. The ex-Midland depot on the right was named so purely because engines from that company visited the building in pre-Grouping days. Both sheds, although of different design, were of NER ownership.
Photomatic

An unidentified Class J77 0-6-0T with round-topped cab outside the NER roundhouse at York South in prewar days with the ex-GNR shed visible on the right. Whilst still of LNER ownership, this latter shed became the 'LMS' stable and was coded 19F up to 1939 when its allocation was withdrawn. W. Potter

'J25' 0-6-0 No 65698 (50A) in store at York South in 1959. For other than stored locos, South shed was the domicile of the pilot engines up to 1961 (as verified by the accompanying views). B. Morrison

50B LEEDS NEVILLE HILL

Pre-Grouping Origin: NER
Gazetteer Ref: 21 D3
Closed: 1966
Shed-Codes: 50B (1949-1960)
55H (1960-1966)
Allocations: 1950 (50B)

Class A3 4-6-2
60036 *Colombo*
60074 *Harvester*
60081 *Shotover*
60084 *Trigo*
60086 *Gainsborough*

Class B1 4-6-0
61035 *Pronghorn*
61062
61065
61069
61216
61218
61237 *Geoffrey H. Kitson*
61240 *Harry Hinchcliffe*
61256   61258   61338
61257   61259   61339

Class B16 4-6-0
61410	61415	61431	61445	61471
61411	61425	61432	61446	61478
61412	61427	61433	61447	
61413	61428	61440	61469	
61414	61429	61442	61470	

Class D49 4-4-0
62739 *The Badsworth*
62746 *The Middleton*
62748 *The Southwold*
62756 *The Brocklesby*
62775 *The Tynedale*

Class Q6 0-8-0
63362   63450

Class J39 0-6-0
64791	64850	64920	64934	64949
64819	64863	64921	64943	

Class J21 0-6-0
65041	65067	65118
65062	65076	65122

Class G5 0-4-4T
67240	67266	77290	67308	67337
67262	67274	67293	67319	

Class J77 0-6-0T
68395   68406

Class J72 0-6-0T
68672   68677   68681

Class N13 0-6-2T
69114   69115   69117   69118

Total 81

Allocations: 1959 (50B)

Class 2 2-6-2T
41247

Class A3 4-6-2
60036 *Colombo*
60074 *Harvester*
60081 *Shotover*
60084 *Trigo*

Class B1 4-6-0
61016 Inyala
61035 *Pronghorn*
61038 *Blacktail*
61062

Neville Hill as rebuilt and viewed from the west in the 1960s.   W. T. Stubbs

Class Q6 0-8-0 No 63417 (55H) inside Neville Hill in 1964. N. Skinner

The last surviving Class N13 0-6-2T, No 69114 (50B) inside its home depot, Neville Hill, in 1955. This ex-Hull & Barnsley Railway loco was scrapped in the following year. B. Morrison

61216
61218
61237 *Geoffrey H. Kitson*
61240 *Harry Hinchcliffe*
61257
61259

Class B16 4-6-0

61411	61415	61428	61432	61447
61412	61425	61429	61442	61470
61414	61427	61431	61446	61471

Class J39 0-6-0

64725	64835	64870	64933	64943
64730	64850	64920	64934	
64758	64863	64922	64935	

Class 3 2-6-0

77004	77013

Class 4 2-6-4T

80116	80117	80118	80119	80120

Class WD 2-8-0

90026	90045	90467	90663

Total 54

Allocations: 1965 (55H)

Class 4MT 2-6-4T

42184	42196	42689	42699

Class 4MT 2-6-0

43054	43075

Class A1 4-6-2
60118 *Archibald Sturrock*
60131 *Osprey*
60134 *1 Foxhunter*
60154 *Bon Accord*

Class K1 2-6-0
62007

Class Q6 0-8-0

63344	63417	63420	63426

Total 15

In 1958 two of the depot's roundhouses were re-roofed and the remaining two were demolished in favour of diesel accommodation.

The shed was re-coded 55H in January 1960.

The shed closed to steam in June 1966 and the remaining engines transferred to Normanton 55E, Low Moor 56F and Leeds Holbeck 55A.

@ 1933

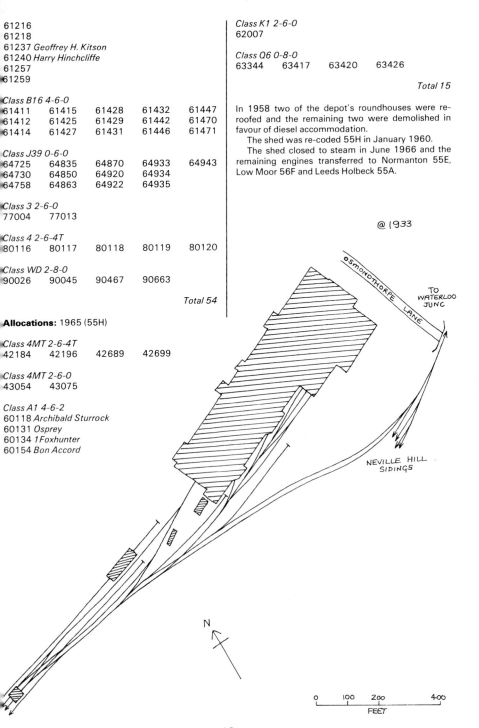

OSMONDTHORPE LANE

TO WATERLOO JUNC

NEVILLE HILL SIDINGS

N

0	100	200	400
FEET

The re-roofing of Neville Hill is well underway in this 1958 view of the depot. Part of the old building can be seen on the left.   IAL

'B16' 4-6-0 No 1418 (eventual BR No 61418) portrayed in the yard at Neville Hill in 1947 with the coaler visible in the background.
LGRP courtesy David & Charles Ltd

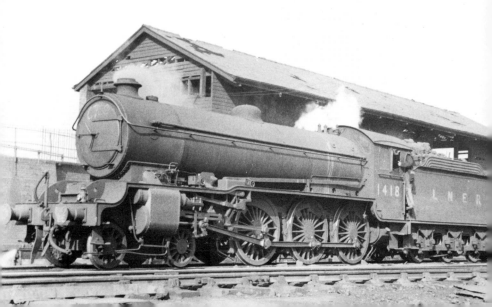

50C SELBY

Pre-Grouping Origin: NER
Gazetteer Ref: 21 D5
Closed: 1959
Shed-Code: 50C (1949-1959)
Allocations: 1950

Class D20 4-4-0
62340	62361	62374	62381	62395
62341	62363	62376	62382	
62348	62366	62378	62386	

Class Q5 0-8-0
63280	63285	63319	63336

Class Q6 0-8-0
63348	63387	63408	63436	63449
63378	63395	63429	63440	63451
63382	63406	63431	63448	63456

Class J21 0-6-0
65039	65042	65105

Class J27 0-6-0
65793	65844	65874	65881	65891
65827	65848	65875	65882	

Class G5 0-4-4T
67250	67286

Class Y1 0-4-0T
68143

Class Y3 0-4-0T
68156	68158	68161

Class J71 0-6-0T
68268

Class J73 0-6-0T
68356	68357	68362

Class J77 0-6-0T
68399	68433

Class A8 4-6-2T
69867	69879

Class Q1 0-8-0T
69931	69933

Total 60

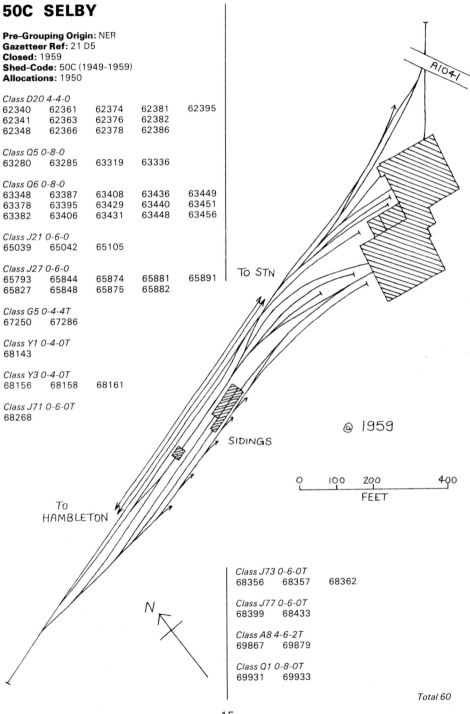

A1041

TO STN

@ 1959

SIDINGS

0   100   200   400
FEET

To
HAMBLETON

N

Allocations: 1959

Class 4 2-6-0

43051	43054	43071	43097	43123
43052	43057	43096	43098	43125

Class 3F 0-6-0T
47634

Class B16 4-6-0

61433	61458	61466
61456	61459	61469

Class Q6 0-8-0

63348	63423	63436	63449	63451
63395	63429	63448	63450

Class J39 0-6-0

64860	64904

Class J25 0-6-0

65663	65685

Class J27 0-6-0

65861	65881	65885	65888	65891

Class Y1 0-4-0T
68150

Class J71 0-6-0T
68275

Class J72 0-6-0T
68686

Class J50 0-6-0T
68948

Class T1 4-8-0T

69910	69912	69921

Total 42

Selby shed closed in October 1959 and the allocation was transferred to 11 other NE region depots, York 50A being the main recipient.

A group of locos around one of Selby's turntables in 1948. H. C. Casserley

A view of the north-easterly entrance to Selby shed from the nearby road-bridge in 1949.
LGRP courtesy David & Charles Ltd

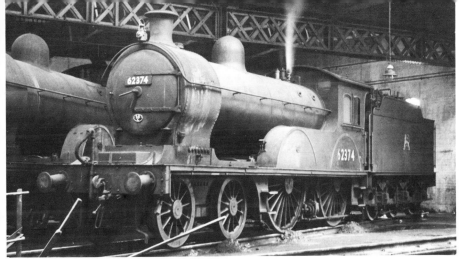

Class D20 4-4-0 No 62374 of Selby inside its home depot in 1954.   B. Morrison

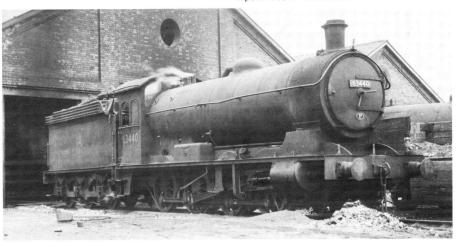

Class Q6 0-8-0 No 63440 (50C) outside the southernmost roundhouse at Selby in 1954.
B. Morrison

Selby shed and yard in 1963, four years after closure, with the tracks given up for coal storage.
W. T. Stubbs

50D Starbeck

Pre-Grouping Origin: NER
Gazetteer Ref: 21 C3
Closed: 1959
Shed-Code: 50D (1949-1959)
Allocations: 1950

Class D20 4-4-0
62342	62370	62384	62392
62343	62373	62389	62397

Class D49 4-4-0
62738 The Zetland
62749 The Cottesmore
62752 The Atherstone
62753 The Belvoir
62755 The Bilsdale
62758 The Cattistock
62762 The Fernie
62763 The Fitzwilliam
62765 The Goathland
62768 The Morpeth
62772 The Sinnington
62773 The South Durham

Class J39 0-6-0
64706	64855	64860	64922	64944
64818	64857	64861	64938	
64845	64859	64866	64942	

Class G5 0-4-4T
67253	67284	67289

Class J77 0-6-0T
68392	68393	68404	68434	68438

Class A6 4-6-2T
69791	69793	69794	69797

Total 45

Allocations: 1959

Class 4 2-6-4T
42477	42553	42639

Class 3F 0-6-0T
47438	47462	47581

Class B16 4-6-0
61478

The southerly end of Starbeck loco in 1949 with none of the four 0-6-0 types portrayed as yet displaying any BR identity.
LGRP courtesy David & Charles Ltd

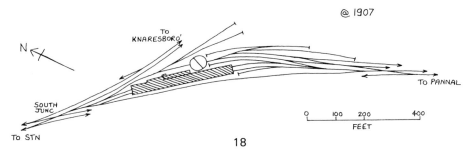

The rebuilt and shortened Starbeck as viewed from the north-west in August 1959, a few weeks before closure. K. Fairey

Class D49 4-4-0 No 62727 The Quorn *(50D) at rest outside Starbeck in 1955.* A. G. Ellis

Class D49 4-4-0
62727 *The Quorn*
62738 *The Zetland*
62753 *The Belvoir*
62759 *The Craven*
62763 *The Fitzwilliam*
62765 *The Goathland*

Class J39 0-6-0

64706	64845	64857	64866
64818	64847	64859	64942
64821	64855	64861	64944

Class J25 0-6-0
65726

Class WD 2-8-0

90044	90054	90457	90518

Total 30

Starbeck shed closed in September 1959 and its allocation was divided between York 50A, Goole 53E, Wakefield 56A, Mirfield 56D, Hull Dairycoates 53A and Sunderland 52G.

'D20' 4-4-0 No 62373 (50D) at Starbeck in 1949.
LGRP courtesy David & Charles Ltd

*Another Class D49 'Hunt' 4-4-0 namely No 62771
The Rufford (50A) on a visit to Starbeck in 1958.
T. Wright*

20

50E SCARBOROUGH

Pre-Grouping Origin: NER
Gazetteer Ref: 22 A3
Closed: 1963
Shed-Code: 50E (1949-1963)
Allocations: 1950

Class 4MT 2-6-0
43052

Class D49 4-4-0
62751 *The Albrighton*
62764 *The Garth*
62769 *The Oakley*
62770 *The Puckeridge*

Class J39 0-6-0
64919   64935

Class J72 0-6-0T
69016

Class A8 4-6-2T
69877   69881   69882   69885   69886

Total 13

Allocations: 1959

Class B16 4-6-0
61445

Class D49 4-4-0
62739 *The Badsworth*
62762 *The Fernie*
62770 *The Puckeridge*

Class J72 0-6-0T
68739

Class A8 4-6-2T
69867   69877   69885

Class 5 4-6-0
73167   73168   73169   73170

Class 3 2-6-2T
82026   82028

Total 14

Scarborough shed was scheduled to close on 19 May 1963 but the last allocated engine No 77004 was transferred to York 50A on 22 April the same year. The withdrawn stock was removed in the May but the shed continued to service locos working in with excursions for some years afterwards.

Scarborough shed in 1959 shortly before the demolition of the left hand portion of the building due to subsidence.   K. Fairey

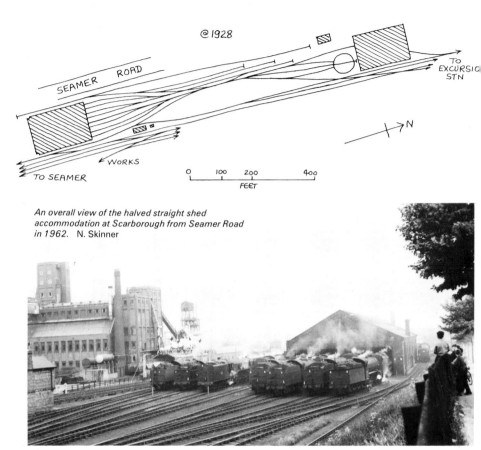

@ 1928

SEAMER ROAD

TO EXCURSION STN

N

WORKS

TO SEAMER

0   100   200   400
FEET

An overall view of the halved straight shed
accommodation at Scarborough from Seamer Road
in 1962.   N. Skinner

Class J39 0-6-0 No 64857 (50D) stands in the
demolished half of Scarborough in 1959. Part of the
depot's notice board can be seen in the distance.
N. Skinner

Scarborough in pre-Grouping days.
H. C. Casserley collection

Class A8 4-6-2T Nos 69867 (left) and 69877 (both 50E) in store in the diminutive roundhouse at Scarborough in 1959. K. Fairey

One of Holbeck's 'Jubilee' class 4-6-0s No 45593 Kolhapur on the turntable outside Scarborough's roundhouse in June 1965. As stated in the text, the shed continued to service excursion motive power well after the 1963 closure. N. Skinner

50F MALTON

Pre-Grouping Origin: NER
Gazetteer Ref: 22 B5
Closed: 1963
Shed-Code: 50F (1949-1963)
Allocations: 1950

Class D49 4-4-0
62774 *The Staintondale*

Class J24 0-6-0
65600   65636   65642
65631   65640   65644

Class E4 2-4-2T
67155

Class G5 0-4-4T
67273   67275   67330   67332   67349

Class Y1 0-4-0T
68147   68150

Class Y3 0-4-0T
68157

Total 16

Allocations: 1959

Class 2 2-6-2T
41251   41265

Class J39 0-6-0
64867   64928   64938

Class J27 0-6-0
65827   65844   65848   65849

Class A8 4-6-2T
69861   69886

Class 3 2-6-2T
82027   82029

Total 13

Of the 1950 allocation Nos 62774 and 68157 were based at Pickering, a sub-shed of Malton, but both locos bore 50F plates and are thus included in the latter depot's complement.

At closure in April 1963, eight locos transferred to York 50A and one went to Goole 50D.

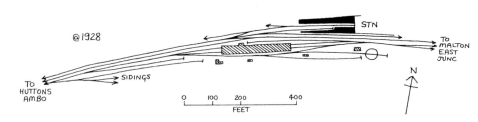

The western approaches to Malton in 1949 with the station in the background.
LGRP courtesy David & Charles Ltd

Malton shed from the east in June 1963, two
months after closure.   W. T. Stubbs

Class A8 4-6-2T No 69886 (50F) outside the
eastern end of Malton in 1958.   T. Wright

Class G5 0-4-4T No 67248 (50F) stands between
the coaling crane and Malton station platform in
1958.   T. Wright

50G WHITBY

Pre-Grouping Origin: NER
Gazetteer Ref: 28 F2
Closed: 1959
Shed-Code: 50G (1949-1959)
Allocations: 1950

Class J24 0-6-0
65621   65624   65627   65628

Class G5 0-4-4T
67302   67335

Class A8 4-6-2T
69858   69861   69865   69890
69860   69864   69888

Total 13

Whitby shed closed on 6 April 1959 and its five remaining engines were dispersed as follows: Nos 42083 and 42085 to York 50A, 42084 to Low Moor 56F and Nos 77004 and 77013 to Leeds Neville Hill 50B.

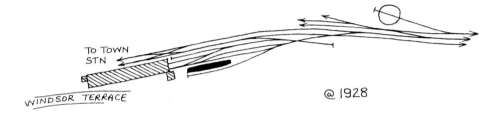

@ 1928

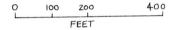

Whitby shed in 1957 on the occasion of a society visit with BR Class 3 2-6-0 No 77013 (50G) on the right. *Real Photos*

26

An array of spotless NER classes at Whitby yard
around the turn of the century.
LGRP courtesy David & Charles Ltd.

Whitby depot from track level in 1949 with most of
the locos still bearing LNER insignia.   B. Hilton

*Class J25 0-6-0 No 65648 (50G) in Whitby yard in
1958.*   T. Wright

*Class A8 4-6-2T No 69865 (50G) at Whitby in 1957
in which year the number of these engines allocated
to this depot had been reduced to two.*   Real Photos

51A DARLINGTON

Pre-Grouping Origin: NER
Gazetteer Ref: 28 E5
Closed: 1966
Shed-Code: 51A (1949-1966)
Allocations: 1950

Class 4MT 2-6-0
43050	43054	43071
43051	43055	43072

Class A3 4-6-2
60070 Gladiateur
60076 Galopin

Class B1 4-6-0
61021 Reitbok
61022 Sassaby
61023 Hirola
61039 Steinbok
61173	61224	61274	61289
61176	61255	61275	61291
61198	61273	61276	

Class K1 2-6-0
62004	62044	62048	62057	62062
62006	62045	62049	62058	
62008	62046	62050	62059	
62009	62047	62056	62061	

Class J39 0-6-0
64710   64933

Class J21 0-6-0
65033	65068	65098	65119
65038	65090	65110	

Class J25 0-6-0
65648	65672	65691	65702
65650	65677	65692	65720
65664	65688	65696	

Class G5 0-4-4T
67272   67333   67342

Class L1 2-6-4T
67742   67750   67754   67777

Class J94 0-6-0ST
68008	68027	68045	68051
68015	68039	68047	68052
68025	68043	68050	

Class Y1 0-4-0T
68136S
68153S

Class J71 0-6-0T
68231	68236	68259	68281	68308
68235	68239	68279	68300	

Class J77 0-6-0T
68408   68410   68423   68432

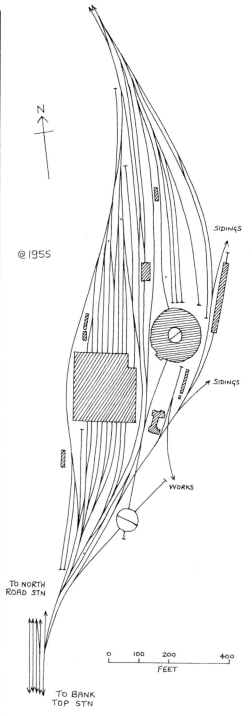

@ 1955

SIDINGS

SIDINGS

WORKS

TO NORTH ROAD STN

TO BANK TOP STN

N

FEET

0   100   200   400

The southerly end of Darlington shed in 1959 with Class B1 4-6-0 No 61024 Addax (51A) *nearest the camera.* P. J. Kelley

Darlington from the south in 1964. W. T. Stubbs

The old shed at Darlington in 1938, a year before it was replaced by the modern through road depot. LGRP courtesy David & Charles Ltd

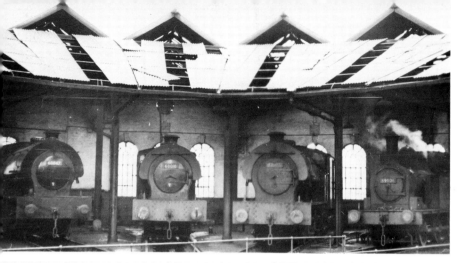

The interior of Darlington roundhouse in 1963 with (left to right) Classes J94 0-6-0ST Nos 68047, 68010, 68025 and J72 0-6-0T 69006 (all 51A). N. Skinner

Class J94 0-6-0ST No 68052 (51A) at the north end of Darlington in 1958.   T. Wright

Class J72 0-6-0T			
68679	68707	69004	

Class N9 0-6-2T			
69426			

Class A5 4-6-2T				
69830	69833	69836	69838	69840
69832	69835	69837	69839	69841

Class WD 2-8-0			
90061	90078	90423	90449	90467

Total 112

Allocations: 1959

Class 4 2-6-0	
43050	43129

Class 2 2-6-0				
46473	46474	46475	46477	46479

Class A3 4-6-2
60053 Sansovino
60058 Blair Athol

Class V2 2-6-2
60848

Class B1 4-6-0				
61176	61229	61276	61321	61382
61198	61273	61291	61338	61387
61224	61274	61319	61353	

Class K1 2-6-0				
62004	62007	62009	62045	62059
62005	62008	62043	62058	62064

Class J27 0-6-0
65860

Class L1 2-6-4T				
67742	67750	67755	67763	67777

Class J94 0-6-0ST				
68007	68017	68027	68043	68050
68008	68024	68037	68045	68052
68015	68025	68039	68047	

Class J72 0-6-0T			
68679	68754	69021	
68716	69004	69022	

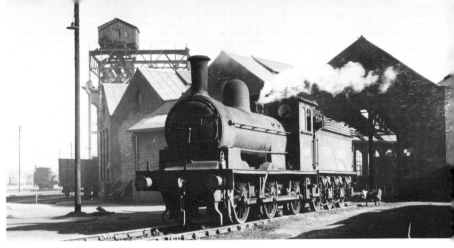

Class J25 0-6-0 No 65688 (51A) outside the
southerly entrance to Darlington roundhouse in
1954. B. Morrison

'Q6 0-8-0 No 63444 (54C) alongside the coaler at
Darlington in 1956. T. Wright

Class J50 0-6-0T				
68897	68898	68909	68934	68959

Class A8 4-6-2T				
69887				

Class WD 2-8-0				
90135	90406	90593	90698	

Total 70

Allocations: 1965

Class 4MT 2-6-4T		
42085	42194	42477

Class 4MT 2-6-0		
43050	43057	43102
43056	43099	43129

Class A1 4-6-2
60124 Kenilworth

Class V2 2-6-2		
60806	60884	60885

Class B1 4-6-0
61216

Class K1 2-6-0				
62001	62008	62043	62045	6205
62003	62041	62044	62048	6206

Class J27 0-6-0
65859

Class J94 0-6-0ST				
68010	68023	68043	68053	6806
68011	68037	68047	68060	

Class WD 2-8-0		
90011	90014	90309

Total 3

At closure in March 1966, the last few locos went
West Hartlepool 51C and Normanton 55E.

1B NEWPORT

Pre-Grouping Origin: NER
Gazetteer Ref: 28 E4
Closed: 1958
Shed-Code: 51B (1949-1958)
Allocations: 1950

Class Q5 0-8-0
63274

Class Q6 0-8-0

63341	63345	63370	63389	63445
63343	63347	63371	63426	63447
63344	63360	63388	63430	

Class J24 0-6-0
65601   65604

Class J26 0-6-0

65730	65740	65751	65760	65770
65731	65741	65752	65761	65772
65732	65742	65753	65762	65773
65734	65743	65754	65763	65774
65735	65744	65755	65765	65777
65736	65745	65756	65766	65778
65737	65746	65757	65767	
65738	65749	65758	65768	
65739	65750	65759	65769	

Class J94 0-6-0ST

68007	68023	68049	68062
68011	68037	68060	

Class T1 4-8-0T

69910	69913	69917	69921
69911	69916	69919	

Class WD 2-8-0

90014	90081	90373	90461	90503
90016	90089	90426	90462	90517
90027	90090	90434	90465	90605
90045	90091	90446	90475	90625
90054	90098	90451	90481	
90068	90132	90452	90487	
90074	90230	90457	90488	
90076	90273	90459	90500	

Total 109

As will be seen from the allocations, Newport hosted
total of 42 'J26' class 0-6-0's from a possible 50 in
950. When the shed closed in June 1958 as a
result of the opening of Thornaby (see 51L), the
allocations had hardly changed and 80% of the stud
still comprised 'J26' and 'WD' locos.
    The entire allocation transferred to Thornaby 51L
upon closure.

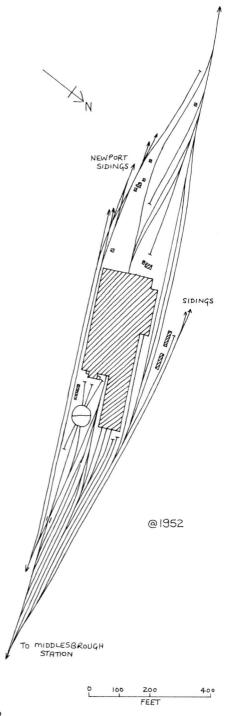

NEWPORT SIDINGS

SIDINGS

@1952

To MIDDLESBROUGH STATION

0   100   200   400
FEET

Looking west to Newport shed and yard in 1949.
LGRP courtesy David & Charles Ltd

*Class B16 4-6-0 No 61474 (50A) at rest on one of
the turntable radii at Newport in 1954.*
H. C. Casserley

*One of the many Class J26 0-6-0s allocated to
Newport, namely No 65773, stands at the western
end of the shed in 1957.   P. J. Kelley*

The interior at Newport in 1954. Facing (left to right) are 'J26' 0-6-0 No 65777 and 'T1' 4-8-0T No 69917 (both 51B). B. Morrison

Class T1 4-8-0T No 69921 (51B) replenishing its tanks in Newport shed yard in 1954. B. Morrison

51C WEST HARTLEPOOL

Pre-Grouping Origin: NER
Gazetteer Ref: 28 D4
Closed: 1967
Shed-Code: 51C (1949-1967)
Allocations: 1950

Class D20 4-4-0
62372   62379

Class Q6 0-8-0
63355	63397	63415	63424	63452
63383	63401	63419	63427	63454
63392	63410	63421	63435	63457
63396	63414	63422	63438	

Class J39 0-6-0
64862   64916   64978

Class J26 0-6-0
65747   65748

Class J27 0-6-0
65782	65803	65818	65846
65790	65816	65820	65866

Class G5 0-4-4T
67271	67314	67331
67291	67316	67343

Class J94 0-6-0ST
68042	68054	68056
68053	68055	68057

Class J71 0-6-0T
68233	68258	68290	68301
68244	68263	68291	68302
68248	68276	68295	68306

Class J73 0-6-0T
68355   68358   68359   68364

Class J72 0-6-0T
68683	68685	68694	68703	68716
68684	68692	68697	68711	68734

Class A8 4-6-2T
69852   69862   69863   69871   69893

Total 77

Allocations: 1969

Class 4 2-6-0
43015   43128

Class B1 4-6-0
61061   61267   61275

Class Q6 0-8-0
63383	63397	63414	63421	63440
63391	63410	63415	63422	63454
63392	63412	63419	63438	63457

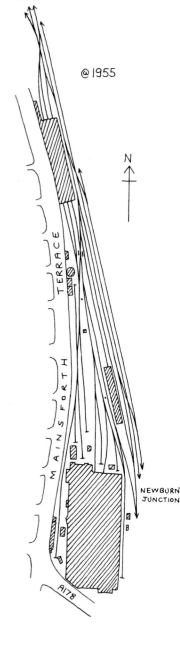

36

The southern end of West Hartlepool's straight shed in 1960.   W. T. Stubbs

The shed yard and entrance to the roundhouse at West Hartlepool in 1959. The coaler is on the extreme left casting its shadow.   W. T. Stubbs

Class J26 0-6-0
65747

Class J27 0-6-0
65782   65816   65820   65846
65805   65818   65830   65866

Class L1 2-6-4T
67765

Class J94 0-6-0ST
68021   68053   68055   68057
68051   68054   68056

Class J71 0-6-0T
68233

Class J73 0-6-0T
68359   68364

Class J77 0-6-0T
68410

Class J72 0-6-0T
68683   68703   68711   68722
68698   68707   68715   68734

Class J50 0-6-0T
68941   68951

Class A8 4-6-2T
69880   69894

Class WD 2-8-0
90048   90067   90092   90344

Total 57

Allocations: 1965

Class 4MT 2-6-0
43015   43100   43123   43128

Class B1 4-6-0
61220   61257

Class K1 2-6-0
62004

Class Q6 0-8-0

63343	63397	63414	63435	63450
63347	63407	63419	63440	63454
63349	63410	63421	63443	
63361	63412	63432	63446	

Class WD 2-8-0

90016	90445	90588	90621
90082	90479	90593	

Total 32

West Hartlepool shed was one of two depots which survived up to the end of steam traction in the North east district (the other was Sunderland). Thus, on 17 September 1967 the depot's nine remaining steam locos went for scrap (Nos 63344/87 and 90074/76/360/478/627/77/95).

As a point of interest, there was once a depot at East Hartlepool but it closed in 1939 and became used as a wagon repair shop. It survived in this capacity well into BR days as the accompanying photographs shows.

See also Sunderland 54A shed-notes.

Another view of West Hartlepool's three lane shed, again from the south but in 1959. Left to right are 'J72' 0-6-0T No 68711, 'Q6' 0-8-0 No 63457, 'J71' 0-6-0T No 68233 and 'B1' 4-6-0 No 61275 (all 51C).   P. J. Kelley

The interior of West Hartlepool's roundhouse in the last few months of steam operation in 1967.
N. E. Preedy

Part of the old East Hartlepool shed in 1956 still in use as a wagon repair shop (see West Hartlepool shed notes). H. C. Casserley

Class K1 2-6-0 No 62044 (51C) gazes north toward West Hartlepool's coaler in 1967. T. A. Heyes

51D MIDDLESBROUGH

Pre-Grouping Origin: NER
Gazetteer Ref: 28 E4
Closed: 1958
Shed-Code: 51D (1949-1958)
Allocations: 1950

Class Q5 0-8-0
63282   63283   63328   63333

Class Q6 0-8-0
63349   63368   63375   63409   63420
63351   63369   63380   63411   63442
63364   63373   63393   63417   63459

Class J39 0-6-0
64821   64847

Class J25 0-6-0
65687   65710   65726

Class J26 0-6-0
65733   65771   65776
65764   65775   65779

Class G5 0-4-4T
67281   67338

Classes V1 & V3* 2-6-2T
67638   67647   67684*   67686*
67639   67673   67685*   67691*

Class L1 2-6-4T
67755   67763   67765
67759   67764   67766

Class J71 0-6-0T
68260   68303   68307   68312

Class J77 0-6-0T
68409   68414   68422   68425

Class J72 0-6-0T
68688   68690   68713   68740   69006
68689   68712   68721   68754   69019

Total 64

Like Newport 51B, Middlesbrough sheds closed in June 1958 and the entire stud of locomotives was transferred to the new shed at Thornaby 51L.

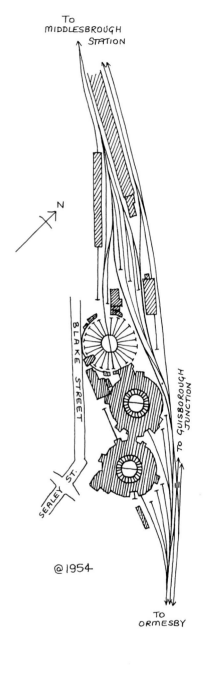

To
MIDDLESBROUGH
STATION

N

BLAKE STREET

SEALEY ST.

TO GUISBOROUGH JUNCTION

@ 1954

TO
ORMESBY

0   100   200   400
FEET

Looking south-east to the non-existent westernmost roundhouse at Middlesbrough shed in 1958, a few months before closure. The outbuildings on the right appear to be the only portion of this part of the depot left standing. B. Hilton

A westerly view of the easternmost building at Middlesbrough in 1954 with a pair of 'Q6' 0-8-0s Nos 63340 (left) and 63373 (both 51D) facing the camera. Photomatic

A trio of Middlesbrough engines at the exposed roundhouse in 1956. Left to right are Classes J72 0-6-0T No 68721, 4MT 2-6-0 No 43073 and Q6 0-8-0 No 63368. T. Wright

Looking west through the interior of the most easterly portion of Middlesbrough shed in 1949. A loco occupies the connecting road to the middle roundhouse.
LGRP courtesy David & Charles Ltd

Class J72 0-6-0T No 68690 (51D) alongside the coaler at Middlesbrough in the mid-1950s.
LGRP courtesy David & Charles Ltd

51E STOCKTON

Pre-Grouping Origin: NER
Gazetteer Ref: 28 E5
Closed: 1959
Shed-Code: 51E (1949-1959)
Allocations: 1950

Class B1 4-6-0
61017 *Bushbuck*
61018 *Gnu*
61030 *Nyala*
61032 *Stembok*
61034 *Chiru*
61037 *Jairou*
61189 *Sir William Gray*
61214   61220   61290   61303

Class K1 2-6-0
62001   62042   62060   62064
62041   62043   62063   62065

Class J25 0-6-0
65689   65718

Class J27 0-6-0
65860   65868   65887

Class G5 0-4-4T
67242   67278   67305   67317   67318

Class V3 2-6-2T
67682

Class Y1 0-4-0T
68144

Class J71 0-6-0T
68305

Class J77 0-6-0T
68407   68412   68420

Class A7 4-6-2T
69781   69787

Class A8 4-6-2T
69883

Class T1 4-8-0T
69918

Class WD 2-8-0
90012   90082   90155   90240   90405
90048   90086   90172   90344   90603
90067   90092   90184   90377   90623

Total 54

Allocations: 1959

Class 4 2-6-0
43073

Class 2 2-6-0
46478

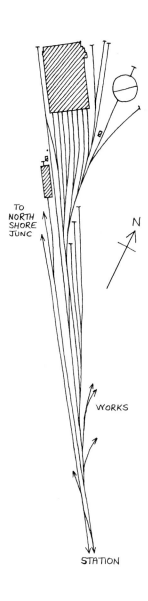

@ 1950

TO
NORTH
SHORE
JUNC

N

WORKS

STATION

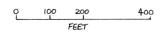

0   100   200   400

FEET

43

Looking north to Stockton shed c1949.
LGRP courtesy David & Charles Ltd

A close-up view of Stockton in 1958 with a pair of the depot's 'K1' 2-6-0s Nos 62060 (left) and 62042.   T. Wright

A redundant Stockton in 1959, two months after closure.   W. T. Stubbs

'G5' 0-4-4T No 7262 (later BR No 67262) of Whitby shed undergoing a service at Stockton in 1947. LGRP courtesy David & Charles Ltd

Class J25 0-6-0 No 5715 at Stockton in 1948. LGRP courtesy David & Charles Ltd

Class B1 4-6-0
61030 *Nyala*
61032 *Stembok*
61034 *Chiru*

61173	61220	61303

Class K1 2-6-0

62001	62041	62047
62003	62042	62065

Class J26 0-6-0
65773

Class J27 0-6-0

65787	65788	65853	65884

Class L1 2-6-4T

67754	67766

Class J94 0-6-0ST
68049

Class J71 0-6-0T
68260

Class J72 0-6-0T
68696

Class J50 0-6-0T
68892

Class WD 2-8-0

90082	90172	90377
90155	90184	90430

Total 31

Stockton shed closed in June 1959 and the bulk of the remaining locos transferred to Thornaby 51L and Darlington 51A.

45

51F WEST AUCKLAND

Pre-Grouping Origin: NER
Gazetteer Ref: 27 E5
Closed: 1964
Shed-Code: 51F (1949-1964)
Allocations: 1950

Class J39 0-6-0
64756   64778   64848

Class J21 0-6-0
65057   65064   65078   65091   65097
65061   65077   65088   65092   65102

Class J25 0-6-0
65659   65671   65683
65662   65675   65706

Class G5 0-4-4T
67294   67312   67345

Class Y1 0-4-0T
68142   68145   68149

Class Y3 0-4-0T
68182

Class J71 0-6-0T
68249   68254   68255   68269

Class J77 0-6-0T
68391

Class J72 0-6-0T
68691   68696   69007

Class A8 4-6-2T
69851   69868   69872
69856   69870   69875

Total 40

Allocations: 1959

Class 2 2-6-0
46482

Class Q6 0-8-0
63340   63353   63403
63351   63398   63459

Looking west to the entrance of West Auckland shed in 1959. W. T. Stubbs

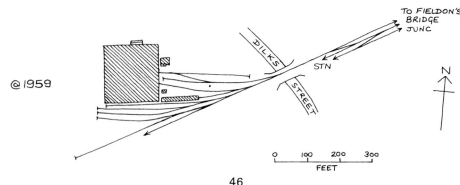

@ 1959

TO FIELDON'S BRIDGE JUNC

DILKS

STN

STREET

N

0   100   200   300
FEET

46

A line-up of Class Q6 0-8-0s at the side of West Auckland shed in 1963 with No 63403 (51F) nearest the camera. N. Skinner

A close-up of West Auckland shed and coaling area in 1954. Photomatic

Class J39 0-6-0
64756	64848	64927	64982
64778	64862	64978	

Class J26 0-6-0
65731	65735

Class J71 0-6-0T
68235	68254	68269

Class J72 0-6-0T
68685	68692	69007
68691	68724	69018

Class A8 4-6-2T
69856

Class 4 2-6-0
76021	76045	76049
76024	76046	76050

Class 3 2-6-0
77002	77003

Class 2 2-6-0
78016

Total 35

West Auckland shed closed in February 1964 and the dozen remaining locos were transferred away. Thornaby 51L received the most (5) but others went to Darlington 51A, Goole 50D, Dairycoates 50B and Stourton 55B.

47

Class J72 0-6-0T No 68692 (51F) in the sidings at West Auckland shed in 1959. N. Skinner

A trio of 0-6-0Ts inside West Auckland shed in 1958 with (left to right) 'J72' No 68685, 'J71' No 68254 and 'J72' No 68691 (all 51F). In all, there were a total of 30 engines 'on shed' this day. B. Hilton

51G HAVERTON HILL

Pre-Grouping Origin: NER
Gazetteer Ref: 28 E4
Closed: 1959
Shed-Code: 51G (1949-1959)
Allocations: 1950

Class Q5 0-8-0
63311   63314

Class Q6 0-8-0
63340   63405   63423   63446
63367   63407   63425   63453
63374   63416   63443

Class J25 0-6-0
65660

Class J27 0-6-0
65787   65830   65855   65865
65805   65853   65859

Total 21

Allocations: 1959

Class B1 4-6-0
61018 *Gnu*
61021 *Reitbok*
61024 *Addax*
61037 *Jairou*
61255

Class Q6 0-8-0
63341   63347   63374   63416   63446
63343   63361   63382   63432
63344   63367   63407   63443

Class WD 2-8-0
90086   90397   90479

Total 21

Haverton Hill shed closed in June 1959 and all bar three of the 1959 listed locos went to Thornaby 51L. The exceptions were 63407/43/46 which transferred to West Auckland 51F.

Haverton Hill shed from the east in 1954. The locos facing are 'J27' 0-6-0 No 65855 (left) and 'K1' 2-6-0 No 62056 (both 51G). Photomatic

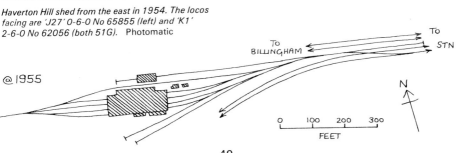

@1955

To BILLINGHAM

To STN

N

0   100   200   300
FEET

49

Class J27 0-6-0 No 65805 at the eastern end of Haverton Hill in 1956.   T. Wright

An overall view of Haverton Hill shed in 1960, a year after closure, with the lanes in use for coal storage. W. T. Stubbs

Class Q5 0-8-0 No 3301 resting at its home depot, Haverton Hill, in June 1948. Although allocated new No 63301, the loco never carried it being withdrawn from service in December the same year. LGRP courtesy David & Charles Ltd

51H KIRKBY STEPHEN

Pre-Grouping Origin: NER
Gazetteer Ref: 27 F2
Closed: 1961
Shed-Code: 51H (1949-1958)
12E (1958)
12D (1958-1961)
Allocations: 1950 (51H)

Class J21 0-6-0
65028	65047	65100
65040	65089	65103

Class J25 0-6-0
65653	65655	65673	65695	65717

Total 11

Allocations: 1959 (12D)

Class 2 2-6-0
46470

Class 4 2-6-0
76020	76023	76051
76022	76047	76052

Class 2 2-6-0
78013	78017	78018	78019

Total 11

Kirkby Stephen became London Midland Region property in February 1958 and took up the code 12E. Further reorganisation found this altered to 12D in April of the same year. The depot closed in November 1961 and the engines moved to Carlisle Canal 12C and Carlisle Upperby 12B.

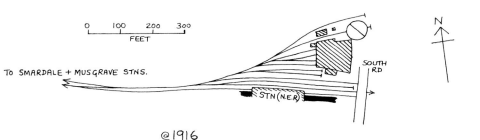

Kirkby Stephen shed in 1953 with 'J25' 0-6-0 No 65655 (51H) on the left. Other locos 'on shed' at the time were (all 51H unless shown otherwise) Nos 46471, 46474, 46476, 46477, 46478, 46480, 65047, 65068 (51A), 65673 and 65695.
B. K. B. Green

A somewhat deserted Kirkby Stephen in 1961, a few months before closure. W. T. Stubbs

A 1958 view of Kirkby Stephen shortly after becoming London Midland Region controlled. BR Standard classes dominate the scene and Class 2 2-6-0 No 78019 (12D) is nearest the camera. B. Hilton

A prewar view of Kirkby Stephen shed in 1935.
H. C. Casserley

Class 2 2-6-0 No 78017 (51H) at Kirkby Stephen in 1957. T. Wright

51J NORTHALLERTON

Pre-Grouping Origin: NER
Gazetteer Ref: 28 G5
Closed: 1963
Shed-Code: 51J (1949-1963)
Allocations: 1950

Class D20 4-4-0
62347   62359   62388   62391

Class J21 0-6-0
65030

Class J25 0-6-0
65645   65693   65725

Class G5 0-4-4T
67324   67344   67346

Class Y3 0-4-0T
68159

Class N10 0-6-2T
69101

Total 13

Allocations: 1959

Class 2 2-6-0
46471

Class K1 2-6-0
62044

Class 2 2-6-0
78010   78011   78012   78014   78015

Total 7

Northallerton was closed in March 1963 and the remaining locos transferred to Darlington 51A.

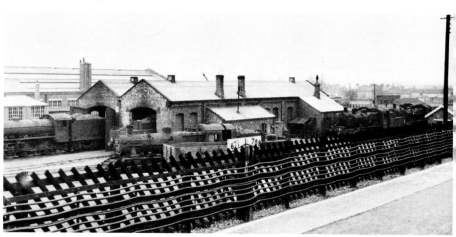

Looking west from the station to the shed at Northallerton in 1957.   B. Hilton

The southern end of Northallerton shed in 1954 with Class J25 0-6-0 No 65726 (51J) outside. Other locos 'on shed' at this time were Nos 62388, 65693, 65720, 67342 and 68159 (all 51J).   B. K. B. Green

close-up of the southern end of Northallerton in
954. Photomatic

The northern end of Northallerton shed in 1937.
H. C. Casserley collection

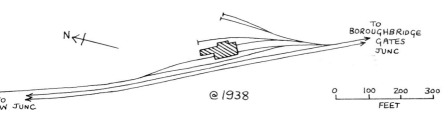

N←↖

TO
BOROUGHBRIDGE
GATES
JUNC

@ 1938

TO
OW JUNC

0   100   200   300
FEET

51K SALTBURN

Pre-Grouping Origin: NER
Gazetteer Ref: 28 E3
Closed: 1958
Shed-Code: 51K (1949-1958)
Allocations: 1950

Class J27 0-6-0
65857

Class A5 4-6-2T

| 69802 | 69811 | 69831 | 69834 | 69842 |

Class A8 4-6-2T

| 69869 | 69884 | 69889 | 69891 | 6989 |

Total 1

Saltburn shed closed in January 1958 and th
remaining engines (Nos 69830/31/34/42/66/6
were reported transferred to Middlesbrough at th
time. This was little more than a paper transaction a
all locos were noted 'in store' at Saltburn in Jun
of the same year. The majority of these wer
withdrawn shortly after but No 69869 is known t
have remained well into 1959 and possibly until i
withdrawal from stock in June 1960.

*Class 5MT 2-6-0 No 42794 (19A) being coaled at
the rear of Saltburn shed in 1955.   K. Fairey*

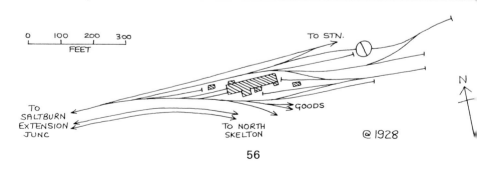

0   100   200   300
FEET

TO STN.

TO
SALTBURN
EXTENSION
JUNC

TO NORTH
SKELTON

GOODS

N

@ 1928

Class A8 4-6-2T No 69883 (51C) being turned at Saltburn in 1955. The shed, although not visible, is to the far left of the loco. A. G. Ellis

One of Saltburn's complement of A5 4-6-2Ts, No 1784, at rest in the shed yard in 1933. LGRP courtesy David & Charles Ltd

51L THORNABY

Origin: BR (NE Region) 1958
Gazetteer Ref: 28 E4
Closed: 1964
Shed-Code: 51L (1958-1964)
Allocations: 1959

Class 4 2-6-0
43072   43102

Class B1 4-6-0
61031 *Reedbuck*

Class Q6 0-8-0
63349	63370	63389	63411	63430
63355	63371	63393	63417	63435
63360	63373	63396	63420	63442
63364	63375	63401	63424	63445
63368	63380	63405	63426	63447
63369	63388	63409	63428	63452

Class J25 0-6-0
65720

Class J26 0-6-0
65732	65745	65757	65768	65777
65736	65751	65760	65769	65778
65737	65753	65761	65772	65779
65741	65755	65762	65774	
65743	65756	65763	65776	

Class J27 0-6-0
65790	65859	65868
65855	65865	65870

Class L1 2-6-4T
67759   67764

Class J94 0-6-0ST
68023   68060   68062

Class J71 0-6-0T
68245   68272

Class J77 0-6-0T
68406

Class J72 0-6-0T
68684	68689	68721	68740	69019
68688	68690	68729	69006	

Class A8 4-6-2T
69860   69869

Class WD 2-8-0
90014	90098	90426	90459	90517
90027	90132	90434	90461	90603
90074	90240	90435	90462	90605
90081	90273	90446	90465	
90090	90373	90451	90481	
90091	90409	90452	90500	

Total 109

Thornaby shed opened in June 1958 and replaced the decrepit establishments at Newport 51B and Middlesbrough 51D. The redundant stock from these latter depots formed Thornaby's initial allocation and the majority were still present the following year as the accompanying list verifies. Despite a schedule to be all-diesel by mid 1962, the shed did not close to steam until December 1964.

The last few engines departed for Darlington 51A, West Hartlepool 51C and Percy Main 52E over a preceding three-month period.

Class Q6 0-8-0 No 63442 (51L) at Thornaby in 1959. A. G. Ellis

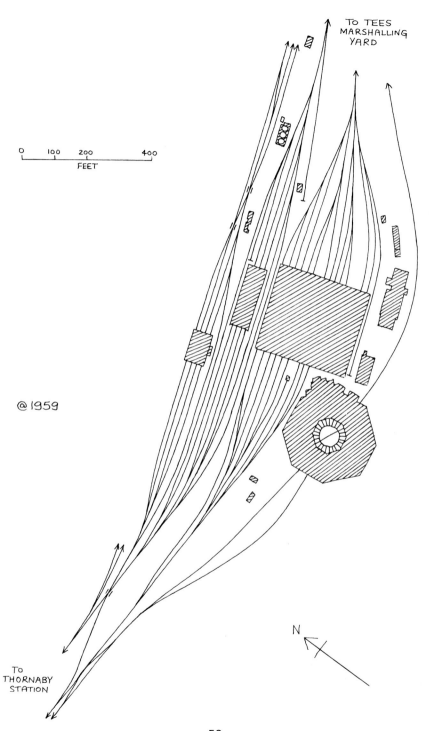

TO TEES
MARSHALLING
YARD

0   100   200   400
        FEET

© 1959

N

To
THORNABY
STATION

Looking east to the main building at Thornaby in 1961. K. Fairey

Class J71 0-6-0T No 68278 (51L) at Thornaby in 1960. N. Skinner

'J26' 0-6-0 and 'Q6' 0-8-0 classes share the metals at the western end of the small four lane 'wash-out' shed at Thornaby in 1962. Left to right are Nos 65755, 63341, 63405 and 65772 (all 51L). B. J. Lynch

he interior of Thornaby's roundhouse after a few
veeks of service in July 1958.   IAL

The westerly entrance to the roundhouse at
Thornaby in 1968, four years after steam closure.
W. T. Stubbs

52A GATESHEAD

Pre-Grouping Origin: NER
Gazetteer Ref: 28 A1
Closed: 1965
Shed-Code: 52A (1949-1965)
Allocations: 1950

Class A4 4-6-2
60001 *Sir Ronald Matthews*
60002 *Sir Murrough Wilson*
60005 *Sir Charles Newton*
60016 *Silver King*
60018 *Sparrow Hawk*
60019 *Bittern*
60020 *Guillemot*
60023 *Golden Eagle*

Class A3 4-6-2
60038 *Firdaussi*
60040 *Cameronian*
60042 *Singapore*
60045 *Lemberg*
60060 *The Tetrarch*
60071 *Tranquil*
60075 *St Frusquin*
60078 *Night Hawk*
60082 *Neil Gow*

Class A1 4-6-2
60115 *Meg Merrilies*
60124 *Kenilworth*
60129 *Guy Mannering*
60132 *Marmion*
60135 *Madge Wildfire*
60137 *Redgauntlet*
60142 *Edward Fletcher*
60143 *Sir Walter Scott*
60145 *Saint Mungo*
60147 *North Eastern*
60150 *Willbrook*
60151 *Midlothian*
60154 *Bon Accord*
60155 *Borderer*

Class A2 4-6-2
60518 *Tehran*
60521 *Watling Street*
60538 *Velocity*

Class V2 2-6-2

60883	60885	60926	60964	60967
60884	60923	60940	60965	

Class B1 4-6-0
61011 *Waterbuck*
61012 *Puku*
61013 *Topi*
61014 *Oribi*
61100
61238 *Leslie Runciman*

Class J39 0-6-0

64701	64707	64869
64704	64853	64871

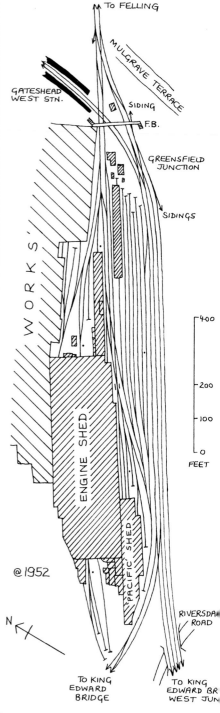

To FELLING

MULGRAVE TERRACE

GATESHEAD WEST STN.

SIDING

F.B.

GREENSFIELD JUNCTION

SIDINGS

WORKS'

400

200

100

0

FEET

ENGINE SHED

'PACIFIC' SHED

@ 1952

N

RIVERSDALE ROAD

To KING EDWARD BRIDGE

To KING EDWARD BR WEST JUN

Class J25 0-6-0 No 65645 (52A) outside the
~~~sterly entrance to the main building at Gateshead
1962. A. G. Ellis

Class N10 0-6-2T		
69090	69092	69100
69091	69097	69109

Total 91

Allocations: 1959

Class A4 4-6-2
60001 *Sir Ronald Matthews*
60002 *Sir Murrough Wilson*
60005 *Sir Charles Newton*
60016 *Silver King*
60018 *Sparrow Hawk*
60019 *Bittern*
60020 *Guillemot*
60023 *Golden Eagle*

~~ss G5 0-4-4T			
309	67320	67325	67329

~~ss V3 2-6-2T		
634	67687	67689
683	67688	67690

~~ss Y1 0-4-0T	
141	68146

~~ss Y3 0-4-0T		
154	68160	68180

~~ss J71 0-6-0T			
251	68270	68283	68309	68314

~~ss J72 0-6-0T			
674	68680	68702	68723	68744
675	68693	68720	68732	69005

The cramped conditions outside the 'Pacific' shed at
Gateshead are well in evidence here in this view
taken c1959. Class A1 4-6-2 No 60157 Great
Eastern (36A) is the loco to the fore. N. E. Preedy

Class A3 4-6-2
60038 *Firdaussi*
60040 *Cameronian*
60042 *Singapore*
60045 *Lemberg*
60051 *Blink Bonny*
60052 *Prince Palatine*
60060 *The Tetrarch*
60070 *Gladiateur*
60071 *Tranquil*
60075 *St Frusquin*
60076 *Galopin*
60078 *Night Hawk*
60091 *Captain Cuttle*

Class A1 4-6-2
60115 *Meg Merrilies*
60124 *Kenilworth*
60129 *Guy Mannering*
60132 *Marmion*
60135 *Madge Wildfire*
60137 *Redgauntlet*
60142 *Edward Fletcher*
60143 *Sir Walter Scott*
60145 *Saint Mungo*
60147 *North Eastern*
60150 *Willbrook*
60151 *Midlothian*
60154 *Bon Accord*
60155 *Borderer*

Class A2 4-6-2
60516 *Hycilla*
60518 *Tehran*
60521 *Watling Street*
60538 *Velocity*

Class V2 2-6-2
60805
60807
60809 *The Snapper, The East Yorkshire Regiment,
       The Duke of York's Own*
60833
60860 *Durham School*
60868   60923   60934   60942   60949
60904   60929   60940   60947   60952
60964 *The Durham Light Infantry*
60967   60979

*Class J72 0-6-0T No 68736 (52A) in North Easter
Railway livery at Gateshead in September 1963. It
will be noted that the roundhouse buildings had be
demolished by this time in readiness for the
conversion of the site to a straight lane structure.
K. Fairey*

Class B1 4-6-0
61012 *Puku*
61022 *Sassaby*

Class J39 0-6-0
64704   64852   64765   64869

Class J25 0-6-0
65656   65700

Classes V1 * & V3 2-6-2T
67637*   67657   67688   67690
67639*   67687   67689

Class J71 0-6-0T
68263   68283   68314

Class J72 0-6-0T
68674   68693   68731   69005
68675   68720   68744   69027
68680   68723   69001

Class N10 0-6-2T
69097   69109

Total *

Allocations: 1965

Class A1 4-6-2
60116 *Hal o' the Wynd*
60127 *Wilson Worsdell*
60129 *Guy Mannering*
60132 *Marmion*
60142 *Edward Fletcher*
60151 *Midlothian*

Class V2 2-6-2

60859	60868	60940	60946	60962
60865	60901	60944	60952	60976

Class B1 4-6-0

61019 *Nilghai*
61035 *Pronghorn*

Total 18

In 1956 Gateshead underwent a facelift; two of the roundhouses fell into disuse and the remaining two were refurbished, one with the provision of a larger 70ft turntable which at long last allowed the Pacific classes to be stabled in the main building. This latter improvement was 30 years too late as 4-6-2 types had been a feature of the depot since the mid-1920s. In the year before closure the site was remodelled yet again, this time with diesels in mind and took the form of a straight lane building.

Although officially closing to steam in March 1965, the locos shown in the (April) 1965 allocation list remained in store at the depot for some months. A good deal of the allocation had gone by the end of 1964, but the final few stored locos departed in October 1965 as follows: Nos 60868/976 to St Margarets 64A and Nos 61019/35 to York 50A.

Class G5 0-4-4T No 67251 (54A) in ex-works condition at Gateshead in 1954.   A. G. Ellis.

Class N10 0-6-2T No 69109 (52A) inside one of the two refurbished roundhouses at Gateshead in 1959.   K. Fairey

*Class N10 0-6-2T No 69092 (52A) at Gateshead in
1954 outside the building which stood to the south-
east of the main yard. The works are visible to the
right of the view.* B. Morrison

*The interior of Gateshead in 1954 whilst still a
quadruple roundhouse with 'V2' 2-6-2 No 60868
(52A) facing.* B. Morrison

52B HEATON

Pre-Grouping Origin: NER
Gazetteer Ref: 28 A1
Closed: 1963
Shed-Code: 52B (1949-1963)
Allocations: 1950

Class 4MT 2-6-0
43070

Class A3 4-6-2
60069 Sceptre
60072 Sunstar
60073 St Gatien
60077 The White Knight
60080 Dick Turpin
60083 Sir Hugo
60085 Manna
60088 Book Law
60091 Captain Cuttle
60092 Fairway

Class A1 4-6-2
60116 Hal o' the Wynd
60126 Sir Vincent Raven
60127 Wilson Worsdell

Class A2 4-6-2
60511 Airborne
60512 Steady Aim
60515 Sun Stream
60516 Hycilla
60517 Ocean Swell
60539 Bronzino

Class V2 2-6-2
60801   60805   60807
60802   60806   60808
60809 The Snapper, The East Yorkshire Regiment,
       The Duke of York's Own
60810   60811   60812   60833
60835 The Green Howard, Alexandra, Princess of
       Wales's Own Yorkshire Regiment
60860 Durham School
60868   60891   60939   60945   60952
60886   60895   60942   60947   60957
60887   60910   60944   60949

Class K3 2-6-0
61818   61901   61917   61962   61985
61875   61904   61930   61969   61986
61884   61906   61952   61984   61987

Class K1 2-6-0
62002   62003   62005   62007   62010

Class J39 0-6-0
64709   64856   64915   64945
64817   64865   64923   64947

Class J27 0-6-0
65788   65842   65864   65886
65800   65862   65869   65889
65807   65863   65873   65893

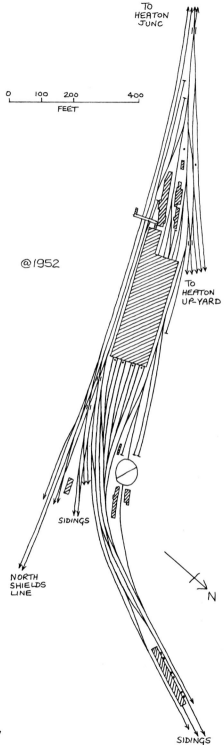

@1952

TO
HEATON
JUNC

TO
HEATON
UP-YARD

SIDINGS

NORTH
SHIELDS
LINE

N

SIDINGS

Class V3 2-6-2T No 67654 (52B) outside the
western end of Heaton shed in 1959. The wall-
mounted watering system with central overhead
outlets for each lane will be noted. K. Fairey

Class V1 2-6-2T				
67635	67640	67642	67646	67652
67637	67641	67645	67651	67654

Class J94 0-6-0ST
68014

Class J71 0-6-0T				
68234	68247	68262	68267	68273
68245	68256	68264	68271	68278

Class J77 0-6-0T
68430

Class J72 0-6-0T				
68682	68687	68725	68738	68742

Class N8 0-6-2T				
69371	69372	69380	69387	69390

Total 119

Allocations: 1959

Class A3 4-6-2
60073 St Gatien
60077 The White Knight
60080 Dick Turpin
60082 Neil Gow
60083 Sir Hugo
60085 Manna
60088 Book Law
60092 Fairway

Class A1 4-6-2
60116 Hal o' the Wynd
60126 Sir Vincent Raven
60127 Wilson Worsdell

Class A2 4-6-2
60511 Airborne
60517 Ocean Swell
60539 Bronzino

Class V2 2-6-2		
60802	60808	60811
60806	60810	60812

60835 The Green Howard, Alexandra, Princess of
Wales's Own Yorkshire Regiment

60846	60901	60932	60962
60886	60910	60944	60976
60891	60922	60945	60978

Class K3 2-6-0			
61818	61875	61923	61984
61844	61884	61927	61986
61869	61906	61962	61987

Class J39 0-6-0				
64701	64853	64871	64926	6494
64703	64856	64915	64931	
64713	64864	64923	64939	

Class J21 0-6-0
65110

Class J27 0-6-0		
65864	65876	65882
65869	65877	65886

Classes V1 and V3* 2-6-2T			
67641	67647	67654*	67683*
67642	67651*	67656*	67685*
67646*	67652*	67658	67691*

Class J94 0-6-0ST
68014

68

Class J72 0-6-0T			
68702	68713	68742	69028
68708	68738	68747	

Total 85

Heaton shed closed in June 1963 and the allocation transferred to Gateshead 52A, Sunerland 52G and Percy Main 52E. The depot remained in use for storage and stabling purposes beyond this date (see photo).

Class V2 2-6-2 No 60860 Durham School *(52A) faces south alongside Heaton's coaler in 1959.* N. Skinner

A trio of 'V3' 2-6-2Ts inside Heaton shed in 1964, a year after official steam closure. The depot's status was more or less a sub-shed of Gateshead at this time, as the locos (left to right) Nos 67646, 67684 and 67638, were all under the direction of 52A. I. S. Carr

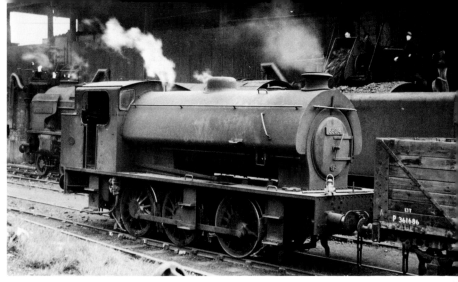

Class J94 0-6-0ST No 68014 (52B) fronts a busy scene at the Heaton coaler in 1954.   B. Morrison

Class J72 0-6-0T No 68702 (52B) takes on water at the eastern end of Heaton shed in 1954.   B. Morrison

52C BLAYDON

Pre-Grouping Origin: NER
Gazetteer Ref: 28 A3
Closed: 1963
Shed-Code: 52C (1949-1963)
Allocations: 1950

Class K1 2-6-0

62021	62023	62025	62027	62029
62022	62024	62026	62028	62030

Class D49 4-4-0
62747 *The Percy*
62771 *The Rufford*

Class Q6 0-8-0

63353	63385	63398	63413	63444
63356	63390	63399	63428	
63376	63391	63403	63432	
63381	63394	63412	63441	

Class J39 0-6-0

64700	64812	64842	64852
64703	64814	64849	64858
64705	64816	64851	64940

Class J21 0-6-0
65025   65082   65099   65111

Class J36 0-6-0
65295   65331   65343

Class G5 0-4-4T

67241	67255	67268	67315
67245	67259	67277	67323
67249	67265	67313	67339

Class V1 2-6-2T

67636	67653	67656	67657	67658

Class J94 0-6-0ST

68010	68024	68036	68048
68019	68029	68038	68058
68021	68035	68041	68059

Class J71 0-6-0T
68265

Class N10 0-6-2T
69095

Total 79

Allocations: 1959

Class B1 4-6-0
61019 *Nilghai*
61100
61238 *Leslie Runciman*

Class K1 2-6-0

62002	62021	62024	62027	62030
62006	62022	62025	62028	
62010	62023	62026	62029	

Class Q6 0-8-0

63352	63363	63381	63394	63441
63356	63376	63385	63399	63453
63362	63378	63390	63413	

Class J39 0-6-0

64812	64815	64842	64858
64814	64816	64849	

Class J21 0-6-0
65033

Class V3 2-6-2T
67634   67636   67653

Class J94 0-6-0ST
68010   68035   68036   68038

Class J72 0-6-0T

68732	69023	69024	69025	69026

Class 3 2-6-0
77011   77014

Total 52

The allocation of Blaydon had been whittled down to 18 locomotives by the official closure date in March 1963, and of these, two-thirds dispersed to

Sunderland 52G, Tyne Dock 52H and North & South Blyth 52F. Five of the remaining six engines lingered until actual closure in June 1963 and were re-allocated as follows: No 61199/237 to Tyne Dock 52H, 63362 to North Blyth 52F, 63437 to Sunderland 52G and 67636 to Gateshead 52A.

71

Class 4 2-6-0 No 43102 (51L) at Blaydon in 1959.
K. Fairey

Blaydon shed from the west c1960.   W. T. Stubbs

One of Blaydon's complement of 'K1' 2-6-0s, No 62027 outside its home depot in 1957.
T. Wright

The interior of Blaydon in 1950 with three Class J39 0-6-0s beside a solitary J94 0-6-0ST. Left to right are Nos 64869, 64703, 64842 and 68058.
H. C. Casserley

Class D49 4-4-0 No 2738 The Zetland alongside the coaler at Blaydon in 1948. The loco was allocated to Gateshead at this time and eventually became BR No 62738. LGRP courtesy David & Charles Ltd

52D TWEEDMOUTH

Pre-Grouping Origin: NER
Gazetteer Ref: 31 D3
Closed: 1966
Shed-Code: 52D (1949-1966)
Allocations: 1950

Class V2 2-6-2
60932

Class B1 4-6-0
61019 *Nilghai*
61024 *Addax*
61025 *Pallah*
61199
61241 *Viscount Ridley*
61322

Class D20 4-4-0

62344	62352	62358	62371
62349	62354	62360	62380
62351	62357	62362	62387

Class J39 0-6-0

64711	64843	64868	64925
64813	64844	64917	64982
64815	64854	64924	

Class J25 0-6-0
65697　65727

Class G5 0-4-4T
67248　67303　67304

Class Y7 0-4-0T
68089

Class J71 0-6-0T
68284

Class J77 0-6-0T
68421　68437

Class WD 2-8-0

90001	90072	90435	90674
90030	90427	90479	90704

Total 47

Allocations: 1959

Class 2 2-6-0
46476

Class A3 4-6-2
60069 *Sceptre*
60072 *Sunstar*

Class V2 2-6-2
60801   60843   60865   60913   60926

Class B1 4-6-0
61014 *Oribi*
61025 Pallah
61199
61241 *Viscount Ridley*
61322

Class K3 2-6-0
61854   61917   61934   61969
61901   61930   61952   61985

Class J39 0-6-0
64711   64844   64916   64925   64949
64813   64868   64917   64929
64843   64897   64924   64941

Class J21 0-6-0
65070

Class J72 0-6-0T
68682   68725

Total 37

Allocations: 1965

Class K1 2-6-0
62006   62021   62025
62011   62023   62050

Class 3MT 2-6-0
77002   77004

Total 8

As Tweedmouth's duties became fewer its allocation was gradually reduced until closure in June 1966 when the last two locos (Nos 77002/4) departed for Stourton 55B.

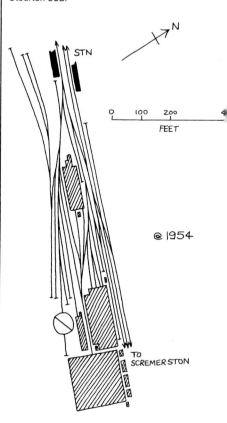

STN

N

0   100   200   4
FEET

@ 1954

TO
SCREMERSTON

The interior of Tweedmouth's roundhouse in 1959 with stored Class D 4-4-0 No 31737 (withdrawn from SR stock 1956). The loco returned to its home territory for restoration soon after.   Photomatic

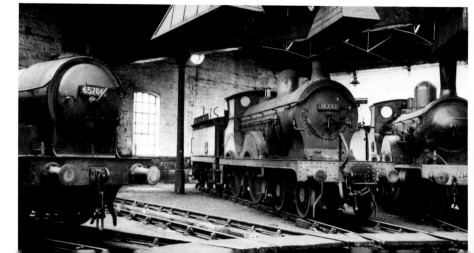

Tweedmouth's straight lane shed from the west in the early 1960s. W. T. Stubbs

Class K3 2-6-0 No 1117 at Tweedmouth in 1933, a year in which the shed possessed nine of these engines. No 1117 was later renumbered 1904 and eventually became BR No 61904 upon nationalisation. LGRP courtesy David & Charles Ltd

Class N8 0-6-2T No 857 in front of the two lane repair shop at Tweedmouth in 1933. The loco did not survive into the BR period although some 30 of its sister engines did. Real Photos

52E PERCY MAIN

Pre-Grouping Origin: NER
Gazetteer Ref: 28 B5
Closed: 1965
Shed-Code: 52E (1949-1965)
Allocations: 1950

Class J27 0-6-0

65780	65795	65812	65822	65838
65784	65796	65813	65825	65839
65791	65802	65814	65826	65852
65792	65806	65815	65831	65858
65794	65809	65821	65837	

Total 24

Allocations: 1959

Class J27 0-6-0

65780	65799	65813	65831	65858
65784	65802	65814	65837	
65791	65807	65821	65839	
65795	65809	65825	65842	
65796	65812	65826	65852	

Total 21

There were few sizeable sheds, if any, that had such a singular allocation as did Percy Main in the BR period. The situation was unchanged at closure in February 1965 when the 14 remaining 'J27s' were dispersed as follows: Nos 65790/95, 65805/09/12/13/14/21/25/42 to South Blyth 52F, Nos 65796, 65802/58 to North Blyth 52F and No 65817 to Sunderland 52G.

TO PERCY MAIN
NORTH JUNC

N

ST JOHN'S STREET

TO
ENGINE
SHED
JUNC

@ 1959

HOWDON
ROAD

0   100   200   300
FEET

An overall view of the depot at Percy Main in 1963 as seen from the St John's street bridge.
J. L. Stevenson

The northern end of the through lane shed at Percy Main in 1954 before complete dilapidation had set in. Photomatic

The dead-end shed at Percy Main in 1959 clearly showing the separate stages of construction. W. T. Stubbs

The south end of the through lane shed at Percy
Main shortly after closure in 1965 with the crude
re-roofing of one lane evident.   W. T. Stubbs

Percy Main through lane shed from the north in
1963 with 11 'J27' 0-6-0s 'on shed'. Those facing
are (left to right) Nos 65795, 65813 and 65802 (all
52E).   V. M. Rayne

52F NORTH & SOUTH BLYTH

Data relating to South Blyth is denoted by an asterisk (*)

Pre-Grouping Origins: NER
Gazetteer Ref: Both 28 A5
Closed: September 1967/May 1967*
Shed-Codes: Both 52F (1949-1967)
Allocations: 1950

Class J21 0-6-0
65035   65080*

Class J27 0-6-0
65781*	65799	65811	65834*	65877
65783	65801	65819	65851	65879
65786	65804	65824*	65867	65880
65789	65808*	65828	65870	65892
65797	65810*	65829*	65876	

Class G5 0-4-4T
| 67244* | 67261* | 67296 | 67334* | 67347• |
| 67246* | 67295* | 67326* | 67341* | |

Class J77 0-6-0T
| 68397 | 68405 | 68424* | 68427 | 68431• |
| 68398 | 68417 | 68426 | 68428* | |

Totals 26
18•

Allocations: 1959

Class J25 0-6-0
65687*   65706*   65727*

Class J27 0-6-0
65781*	65797	65810*	65828	65863
65783	65800*	65811	65834*	65867
65786	65801	65815*	65838*	65875
65789	65804	65819	65851	65879
65792	65806	65822*	65857	65880
65794	65808*	65824*	65862*	65889

Class J77 0-6-0T
68408*

Totals 20
14•

Allocations: 1965

Class 4MT 2-6-0
43140

Class K1 2-6-0
62002*   62022   62024

Class Q6 0-8-0
| 63354 | 63362 | 63386 | 63429 |
| 63359 | 63381 | 63413 | 63459 |

Class J27 0-6-0
65789	65804	65819*	65855*	65880
65790*	65805*	65821*	65858*	65882•
65792	65809*	65825*	65860*	65892
65794	65811	65834	65861*	65893•
65795*	65812*	65838*	65862*	
65796	65813*	65841*	65869	
65801	65814*	65842*	65874*	
65802	65815	65851	65879	

Totals 27
21•

As there was coal traffic on both sides of the river Blyth it was necessary to have engine sheds on the North and South banks to avoid lengthy workings to and fro' via Bedlington. Although North Blyth was marginally senior by virtue of numbers of engines allocated, both depots were coded 52F despite complete independence of each other. Contrary to what one may think, there were very few locomotive transfers between the sheds during the entire BR period.

The respective loco complements at each depot fluctuated with the area's coal output. Scrutiny of 1959 list would therefore suggest that mineral traffic was below peak at this time.

South shed was the first to close in May 1967 and its remaining J27s transferred to Sunderland 52G. North survived until 9 September 1967 — eight days before the end of steam traction in the area. The last five engines (Nos 43000/50/63/70 and 43137) all went for scrap.

The approach to North Blyth shed from the north on a murky day in 1949.
LGRP courtesy David & Charles Ltd

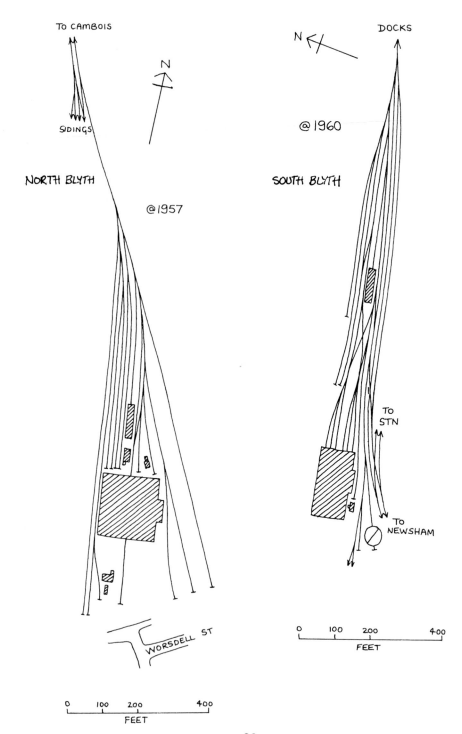

TO CAMBOIS

SIDINGS

NORTH BLYTH

@1957

N

DOCKS

N

@1960

SOUTH BLYTH

TO
STN

TO
NEWSHAM

WORSDELL ST

0 100 200 400
FEET

0 100 200 400
FEET

North Blyth yard in 1963 with 'Q6' 0-8-0 No 63402 (52F) in charge of coaling ramp duties. J. L. Stevenson

Class J27 0-6-0 No 65845 (52F) being replenished at North Blyth's coal stage in 1963. V. M. Rayne

The interior of North Blyth shed in 1965 with the last two Class J72 0-6-0Ts in service, Departmental Nos 58 (left of centre) and 59 (right of centre). The locos' numbers in normal service had been 69005 and 69023 respectively. P. G. Jump

A brace of Class J27 0-6-0s peer out from the shed at South Blyth in 1965. N. Skinner

An overall view of South Blyth in 1963. H. C. Casserley

An early BR view of South Blyth in 1949. LGRP courtesy David & Charles Ltd

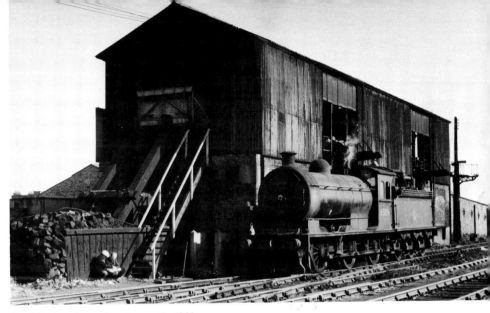

South Blyth coal stage from the west in 1963.
K. Fairey

The interior of South Blyth in 1966 with a monopoly of 'J27' 0-6-0s. Facing (left to right) are Nos 65825, 65814 and 65859 (all 52F). M. S. Welch

53A HULL DAIRYCOATES

Pre-Grouping Origin: NER
Gazetteer Ref: 22 A2
Closed: 1967
Shed-Codes: 53A (1949-1960)
50B (1960-1967)
Allocations: 1950 (53A)

Class 4MT 2-6-0
43053

Class B1 4-6-0

61060	61068	61074	61080

Class K3 2-6-0

61813	61874	61903	61932	61965
61814	61883	61920	61934	
61819	61892	61922	61935	
61871	61899	61923	61941	
61872	61902	61927	61945	

Classes O1 and O4 2-8-0*

63603	63732	63764	63823	63857
63628	63740*	63769	63828	63874*
63664	63753	63770	63835	63881
63673	63754	63772	63845	
63676*	63755*	63812	63855	
63712*	63760*	63816	63856	

Class J39 0-6-0

64864	64897	64927	64939
64867	64914	64928	64941
64870	64926	64931	

Class J25 0-6-0

65647	65654	65690	65699	65713
65651	65663	65698	65712	

Class F4 2-4-2T

67171	67175

Class Y1 0-4-0T

68137	68139	68140

Looking north-east to the straight shed at Dairycoates in 1960 with three Class K3 2-6-0s facing the camera. The locos on the extreme left stand on the site of one of the roundhouses whose buildings had been demolished by this time. K. Fairey

Class J71 0-6-0T

68232	68252	68288	68298	68311
68242	68277	68296	68304	68316

Class J72 0-6-0T

68748	69010	69011

Class N10 0-6-2T

69093	69098	69104	69107
69094	69099	69105	69108
69096	69102	69106	

Class N8 0-6-2T

69377	69382	69389	69398
69379	69385	69392	69401
69381	69386	69393	

Class A7 4-6-2T

69770	69773	69778	69782	69786
69771	69775	69779	69783	69788
69772	69777	69780	69784	

Class T1 4-8-0T

69912	69914	69915	69920	69922

Class WD 2-8-0

90006	90021	90382	90483	90695
90008	90022	90409	90567	
90009	90057	90450	90663	

Total 145

Allocations: 1959 (53A)

Class 4 2-6-0

43053	43076	43078	43099	43122
43069	43077	43079	43103	43131

Class B1 4-6-0

61065	61256

Class K3 2-6-0

61813	61857	61892	61903	61935
61814	61871	61893	61904	61941
61819	61872	61897	61920	61945
61846	61874	61899	61922	61965
61847	61883	61902	61932	

Class J39 0-6-0

64709	64910	64940	64971
64819	64914	64947	

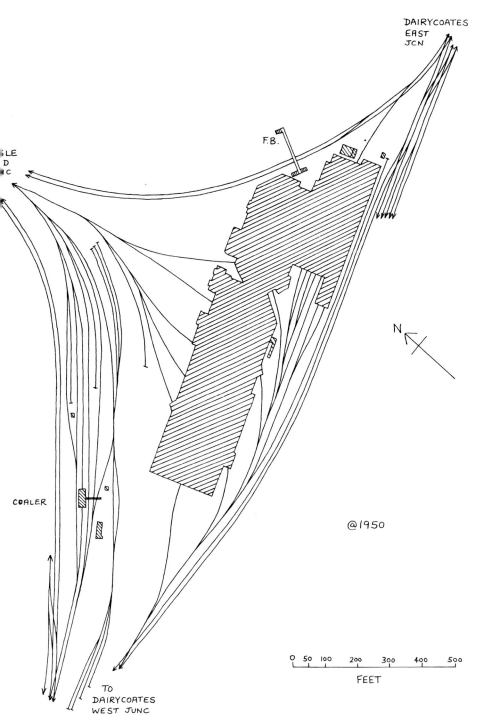

DAIRYCOATES
EAST
JCN

F.B.

LE
D
C

N

@1950

COALER

0 50 100   200   300   400   500
FEET

TO
DAIRYCOATES
WEST JUNC

85

Two Class D49 4-4-0s Nos 62763 The Fitzwilliam
(53A) (left) and 62717 Banffshire *(53B) outside the
straight shed at Hull Dairycoates in 1959.*
N. E. Preedy

*Class J25 0-6-0 No 65693 (left) and '3F' 0-6-0T
No 47580 (both 50B) side by side at one of
Dairycoates' denuded roundhouses in 1960.*
K. Fairey

Class J25 0-6-0				Class 3 2-6-0				
65691	65693			77000	77010			
Class J94 0-6-0ST				**Class WD 2-8-0**				
68011	68042			90006	90072	90352	90511	90677
				90008	90078	90378	90571	90688
Class J71 0-6-0T				90009	90099	90427	90586	90695
68230	68264			90011	90160	90450	90609	90704
				90022	90217	90458	90623	
Class J73 0-6-0T				90030	90233	90482	90627	
68360	68361			90057	90272	90503	90670	
Class J77 0-6-0T								
68409	68425							*Total 94*
				Allocations: 1965 (50B)				
Class J72 0-6-0T								
68670	68741	68752	69008	**Class 4MT 2-6-0**				
68672	68751	68753		43069	43076	43077	43078	43079

An interior view of Dairycoates in 1952 portraying three different tank classes. On the connecting road is 'T1' 4-8-0T No 69922 whilst the two central locos are 69099 and 69093 of class N10 0-6-2T. The right-hand engine is 'N8' 0-6-2T No 69386.
H. C. Casserley

An early LNER illustration of Dairycoates interior with the end of the shed not even visible!
Crown Copyright, National Railway Museum

Sentinel Class Y3 0-4-0T No 68155 (53D) inside Dairycoates in 1954. B. Morrison

Class B1 4-6-0
61010 *Wildebeeste*
61012 *Puku*
61032 *Stembok*

61255	61289	61306

Class WD 2-8-0

90008	90092	90352	90462	90677
90009	90213	90378	90478	90688
90030	90262	90450	90586	90695
90044	90265	90452	90627	90704
90057	90272	90458	90670	

Total 35

Dairycoates was the largest shed on the NE Region and boasted a massive roundhouse with six turntables. It was recoded 50B in January 1960 and the last few steam locos departed upon closure in June 1967.

Looking north-east to the coaling plant at Dairycoates in 1962.   I. S. Carr

*A group of engines around the turntable inside Dairycoates in 1952. Note the chalked instructions to shed staff on the buffers of the locos — this was a particular feature of the depot's operation.
E. D. Bruton*

53B HULL BOTANIC GARDENS

Pre-Grouping Origin: NER
Gazetteer Ref: 22 A1
Closed: 1959
Shed-Code: 53B (1949-1959)
Allocations: 1950

Class B1 4-6-0
61010 *Wildebeeste*
61215 *William Henton Carver*
61304   61305   61306

Class D20 4-4-0
62345   62383   62396

Class D49
62700 *Yorkshire*
62703 *Hertfordshire*
62710 *Lincolnshire*
62720 *Cambridgeshire*
62722 *Huntingdonshire*
62723 *Nottinghamshire*
62734 *Bedfordshire*
62737 *The York and Ainsty*
62741 *The Blankney*
62743 *The Cleveland*
62754 *The Berkeley*
62757 *The Burton*
62767 *The Grove*

Class G5 0-4-4T
67254   67280   67301   67321
67256   67282   67311   67340

Class C12 4-4-2T
67354   67391   67393   67395
67371   67392   67394   67397

Class Y1 0-4-0T
68151

Class J77 0-6-0T
68401

Class A6 4-6-2T
69796   69798

Class A8 4-6-2T
69854   69859   69873   69878   69894
69855   69866   69876   69880

Total 50

Allocations: 1959

Class B1 4-6-0
61010 *Wildebeeste*
61068
61080
61215 *William Henton Carver*
61289   61304   61305   61306

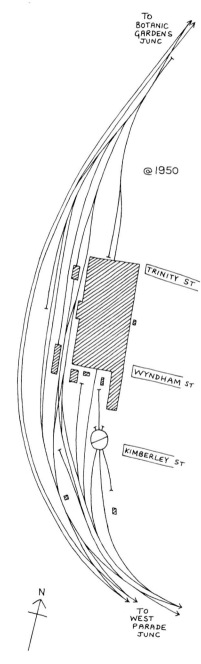

Class D49 4-4-0
62701 *Derbyshire*
62707 *Lancashire*
62710 *Lincolnshire*
62717 *Banffshire*
62720 *Cambridgeshire*
62722 *Huntingdonshire*
62723 *Nottinghamshire*
62760 *The Cotswold*

Classes V1 * & V3 2-6-2T
67635* 67640* 67677 67684
67638 67663 67682 67686

Class J73 0-6-0T
68363

Class 3 2-6-0
77001

Total 26

Hull Botanic Gardens shed was closed to steam in June 1959 despite a major rebuild two years previously. Scarborough 50E received a couple of locos but the majority of the displaced stock went to neighbouring Dairycoates 53A.

Hull Botanic Gardens interior in 1952 with five of its eight Class C12 4-4-2Ts visible and No 67395 nearest. H. C. Casserley

By the mid-1950s Botanic Gardens had become semi derelict as this view shows. Left to right are Nos 67755 (53B), 69881 (50E) and 67337 (53B). B. Hilton collection

Class X2 2-2-4T No 957 inside Botanic Gardens in 1931. This loco was withdrawn from service in 1937. H. C. Casserley

Class D49 4-4-0 No 62724 Bedfordshire *(53B) alongside the coaler at Botanic Gardens in 1954.* B. Morrison

53C HULL SPRINGHEAD

Pre-Grouping Origin: H&BR
Gazetteer Ref: 22 A2
Closed: 1958
Shed-Code: 53C (1949-1958)
Allocations: 1950

Class J25 0-6-0
65667   65705   65728

Class J73 0-6-0T
68360   68361   68363

Class J77 0-6-0T
68402   68413   68429   68435   68440

Class J72 0-6-0T
68670   68686   68746   68752   69002
68673   68724   68747   68753   69003
68676   68743   68751   69001   69009

Class N13 0-6-2T
69111   69112   69113   69116   69119

Class A7 4-6-2T
69774   69776   69785   69789

Class WD 2-8-0
90007   90052   90217   90470   90586
90010   90094   90233   90478   90661
90011   90116   90378   90497   90677
90047   90160   90429   90571   90688

Total 55

This ex-Hull & Barnsley Railway depot was officially closed in December 1958 but the entire allocation (Nos 68360/61, 77000/10, 90011/233/352/78/427/82/503/11/86/623/77/88) moved to Hull Dairycoates 53A at the end of the preceding month.

The shed was occasionally used as a loco storage venue for a couple of years after this date.

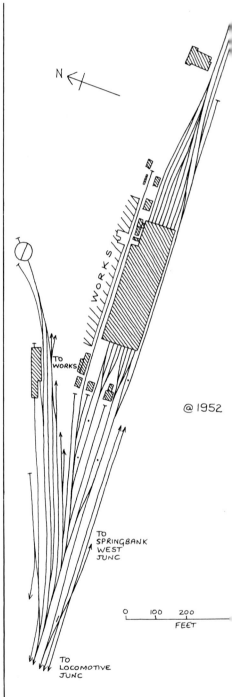

@ 1952

Hull Springhead from the east in 1952. The locos in the centre are (left to right) Classes N13 0-6-2T No 69113, A7 4-6-2T No 69780 and J72 0-6-0T No 69001 (all 53C). N. E. Preedy

Class J71 0-6-0T No 1199 (eventual BR No 68296) at the western end of Springhead shed in 1933 with the coaler visible in the left background. Real Photos

Class J77 0-6-0T No 68429 (53C) inside Springhead in 1950. As will be seen the 'roof' was little more than an unglazed greenhouse by BR days. Real Photos

Ex-Hull & Barnsley Railway Class N13 0-6-2T No 69113 (53C) at Springhead in 1952.
H. C. Casserley

The WD 2-8-0s were the mainstay of Springhead's freight workings during the BR period. Here we see No 90011 (53C) inside the shed in 1956, two years before closure.   A. G. Ellis

53D BRIDLINGTON

Pre-Grouping Origin: NER
Gazetteer Ref: 22 B3
Closed: 1958
Shed-Code: 53D (1949-1958)
Allocations: 1950

Class D20 4-4-0
62353   62355   62365   62375

Class D49 4-4-0
62701 *Derbyshire*
62707 *Lancashire*
62750 *The Pytchley*
62766 *The Grafton*

Class Y1 0-4-0T
68148

Class Y3 0-4-0T
68155

Total 10

Bridlington lost its allocation in June 1958 when the last two locos (Class G5 0-4-4Ts Nos 67280/341) departed for Hull Dairycoates 53A. The shed was officially closed in the following December but continued to turn about excursion visitors for some years afterwards.

Bridlington shed in 1955 with one of its Class D49 4-4-0s, No 62707 Lancashire *occupying the centre road.* K. Fairey

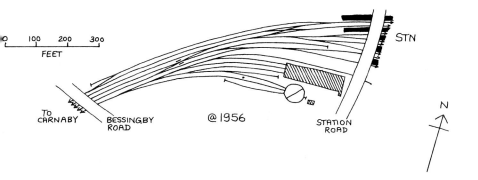

To say that Bridlington handled excursion locos after closure would appear to be something of an understatement in this 1959 portrait. Facing (left to right) are Classes 5 4-6-0 No 44932 (26B), K3 2-6-0 No 61841 (2F), B1 4-6-0 Nos 61111 (41A) and 61036 Ralph Assheton (36A) and V2 2-6-2 No 60855 (50A).   N. Skinner

Class K3 2-6-0 No 61889 (40B) rests at Bridlington shed in 1962 after hauling the 'Doncaster pentecostal Sunday Schools' excursion.   N. Skinner

A 1964 view of Bridlington with Class B1 4-6-0 No 61012 Puku (50B) to the fore. Had this loco's number been illegible, the tell-tale chalk marks on the buffers would have suggested Hull Dairycoates as the home depot (see 53A illustrations).   D. Hardy

53E CUDWORTH

Pre-Grouping Origin: H&BR
Gazetteer Ref: 42 D2
Closed: 1951
Shed-Code: 53E (1949-1951)
Allocations: 1950

Class O4 2-8-0
63620   63667   63751   63843   63849

Class J25 0-6-0
65714

Total 6

By BR days Cudworth shed was a shadow of its former self as much of the ex-Hull & Barnsley system was in decline. It will be noted that if each loco in the accompanying list had acquired a shed-road to itself, there would still have been two lanes vacant!

At closure in July 1951 the six redundant 'O4s' (Nos 63751/54/72/845/49/57) moved to LMR metals at Royston 20C. They were not in residence long and were exchanged for six of Colwick's (38A) WD 2-8-0s a month later. There can have been few locos which found themselves allocated to three different regions in such a short space of time.

@ 1932

To CUDWORTH NORTH JUNC

To CUDWORTH SOUTH JUNC

N

0   100   200   300
FEET

Looking north to the ex-Hull & Barnsley Railway shed at Cudworth in 1925.   Real Photos

Class D24 4-4-0 No 2426 and the water tower at Cudworth as viewed from the west in LNER days. None of this class of loco survived into the BR period.   Real Photos

54A SUNDERLAND

Pre-Grouping Origin: NER
Gazetteer Ref: 28 C5
Closed: 1967
Shed-Codes: 54A (1949-1958)
52G (1958-1967)
Allocations: 1950 (54A)

Class J27 0-6-0
65785	65832	65840	65850	65872
65798	65833	65841	65854	65878
65817	65835	65843	65856	65884
65823	65836	65847	65871	

Class G5 0-4-4T
67243	67258	67270	67300	67348
67247	67260	67276	67307	
67251	67263	67283	67310	
67252	67264	67297	67328	
67257	67267	67298	67336	

Class J94 0-6-0ST
68016

Class J72 0-6-0T
68678	68698	68704	68718	69018

Class N9 0-6-2T
69413	69423	69425
69418	69424	69427

Class A8 4-6-2T
69850	69853	69857	69874	69887

Total 57

Allocations: 1959 (52G)

Class Q7 0-8-0
63464	63466	63467	63474

Class J25 0-6-0
65662	65666

Class J27 0-6-0
65798	65833	65841	65856	65878
65817	65835	65850	65871	65892
65832	65840	65854	65872	

Class V1 2-6-2T
67645   67673

Class J94 0-6-0ST
68016	68041	68044	68048	6805⬛

Class J72 0-6-0T
68678   68704   69002

Class A8 4-6-2T
69850	69854	69858	69873	6987⬛
69852	69855	69859	69874	6988.
69853	69857	69870	69875	6988⬛

Total 4⬛

Allocations: 1965 (52G)

Class K1 2-6-0
62026   62030

Class Q6 0-8-0
63346	63404	63406	63437	6344⬛
63387	63405	63436	63444	6345⬛

Class J27 0-6-0
65788	65832	65853	65873
65817	65833	65865	65885
65831	65835	65872	

Total 2⬛

Sunderland shed was recoded 52G in Septembe⬛
1958 as the group 54 depots came under th⬛
jurisdiction of the Gateshead district.

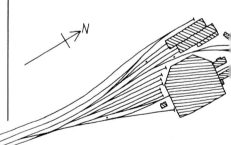

The shed was one of the last two MPDs in the
north-east locality with steam traction (the othe⬛
being West Hartlepool 51C) and closed or
17 September 1967. The final allocations (all t⬛
scrap) were: Nos 63395, 65811/55/79/82/94 an⬛
90009/135/348/78/82/417.

Taking the North Eastern Region as a whole, i⬛
was ironic that the last group of sheds with steam i⬛
the entire region were the ex-LMR depots of th⬛
Leeds district which became NE territory in 1957. A⬛
such, Leeds Holbeck 55A was the very last stea⬛
venue in the region and survived until Novembe⬛
1967 when No 62005 was withdrawn.

Five 'J27' 0-6-0s inside Sunderland's roundhouse in
1967, (left to right) Nos 65879, 65892, 65894,
65811 and 65855.   J. L. Stevenson

Another collection of 'J27' 0-6-0s inside Sunderland
in 1967, (left to right) Nos 65880, 65892, 65795,
65804, 65894 and 65855.   N. E. Preedy

The two straight sheds at Sunderland in 1950 prior
to the BR rebuild. One of the shed's large allocation
of 'G5' 0-4-4Ts at the time, No 67252, stands
outside.   H. C. Casserley

An overall view of Sunderland MPD from the south in 1963.   K. Fairey

The rebuilt straight sheds at Sunderland in 1959.
P. J. Kelley

Class J39 0-6-0 No 64851 (withdrawn from service in December 1962) at Sunderland in 1963 awaiting its call to the scrapyard.   I. S. Carr

54B TYNE DOCK

Pre-Grouping Origin: NER
Gazetteer Ref: 28 B5
Closed: 1967
Shed-Codes: 54B (1949-1958)
52H (1958-1967)
Allocations: 1950 (54B)

Class Q6 0-8-0
63352   63363   63379   63437

Class Q7 0-8-0
63460   63463   63466   63469   63472
63461   63464   63467   63470   63473
63462   63465   63468   63471   63474

Class J25 0-6-0
65666   65670   65694   65716

Class G5 0-4-4T
67288

Class Y3 0-4-0T
68181   68183

Class J71 0-6-0T
68266   68272

Class J72 0-6-0T
68706   68729   68731   69008

Class N8 0-6-2T
69378   69400

Class N9 0-6-2T
69410   69429

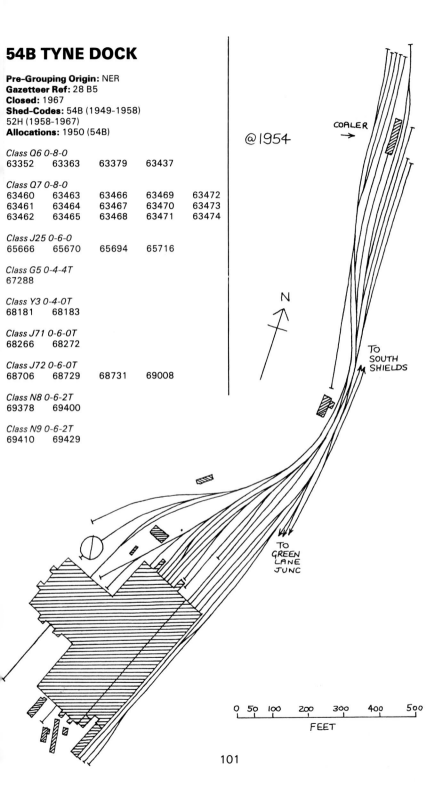

@1954

COALER →

N

TO
SOUTH
SHIELDS

TO
GREEN
LANE
JUNC

0 50 100   200   300   400   500
FEET

Class WD 2-8-0

90026	90309	90445	90485
90210	90352	90458	90611
90272	90430	90482	90627

Total 48

Allocations: 1959 (52H)

Class Q6 0-8-0

63387	63425	63437

Class Q7 0-8-0

63460	63463	63469	63472
63461	63465	63470	63473
63462	63468	63471	

Class O1 2-8-0

63712	63755	63760	63856	63874

Class J21 0-6-0
65099

Class J25 0-6-0

65645	65670	65695	65713

Class J94 0-6-0ST

68029	68031	68059

Class J71 0-6-0T

68262	68265

Class J72 0-6-0T

68706	68743

The entrance to the eastern-most portion of Tyne Dock shed in 1954. Photomatic

Class N10 0-6-2T

69101	69105

Class T1 4-8-0T
69917

Class 9F 2-10-0

92060	92062	92064	92066	92098
92061	92063	92065	92097	92099

Total 44

Allocations: 1965 (52H)

Class B1 4-6-0
61199

Class Q6 0-8-0

63360	63371	63389	63411
63363	63377	63398	63431
63366	63384	63409	63453

Class WD 2-8-0

90434	90459

Class 9F 2-10-0

92060	92062	92064	92066	92098
92061	92063	92065	92097	92099

Total 25

Tyne Dock was re-coded 52H in September 1958.

The shed closed on 9 September 1967 and its final allocation of Class K1 2-6-0's were dispersed as follows: No 62005 to Leeds Holbeck 55A and Nos 62007/11/45/50 to scrap. No 62005 had the distinction of being the sole surviving engine on the North Eastern Region and was withdrawn in November 1967 (see 54A notes). The loco is now preserved and can be seen on the North Yorkshire Moors Railway which connects Grosmont and Pickering.

Class T1 4-8-0T No 69921 (52H) framed in the rear entrance to the westerly roundhouse at Tyne Dock in 1959. P. J. Kelley

A pair of Class Q6 0-8-0s Nos 63377 (left) and 63363 (both 52H) inside a roofless Tyne Dock in 1963. K. Fairey

Another view of the dilapidation at Tyne Dock by 1963 with 'Q6' 0-8-0 No 63393 (52H) within. K. Fairey

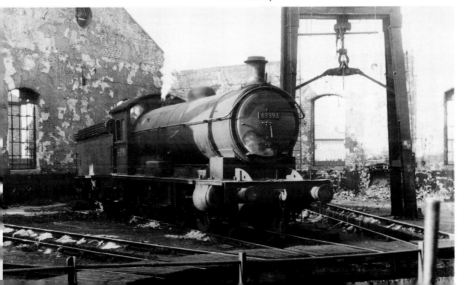

Class Q6 0-8-0 No 63359 (54B) looks north outside the westerly roundhouse at Tyne Dock in 1954. B. Morrison

The interior of Tyne Dock in 1954 depicting 'J25' 0-6-0 No 65694 (54B) shortly before its withdrawal. B. Morrison

54C BOROUGH GARDENS

Pre-Grouping Origin: NER
Gazetteer Ref: 28 A1
Closed: 1959
Shed-Codes: 54C (1949-1958)
52J (1958-1959)
Allocations: 1950 (54C)

Class B1 4-6-0
61319   61320   61321

Class Q5 0-8-0
63251   63259   63267   63284   63303
63257   63261   63271   63287   63326

Class Q6 0-8-0
63342   63358   63384   63402
63350   63366   63386   63434
63354   63377   63400   63458

Class J39 0-6-0
64846   64929   64936

Class J24 0-6-0
65611   65615

Class J25 0-6-0
65657   65676   65685
65661   65680   65686

Class J71 0-6-0T
68287   68289   68299

Class J72 0-6-0T
68705   68728   68736   69017
68708   68730   68737

Class N8 0-6-2T
69391

Total 47

Allocations: 1959 (52J)

Class K1 2-6-0
62060

Class Q6 0-8-0
63342   63358   63386   63431   63458
63346   63366   63400   63434
63350   63377   63402   63444
63354   63384   63408   63456

Class J39 0-6-0
64700   64710   64851   64921
64707   64846   64854   64936

Class J25 0-6-0
65702   65712   65728

Class J27 0-6-0
65785   65823   65847   65873   65893

Class J71 0-6-0T
68278   68316

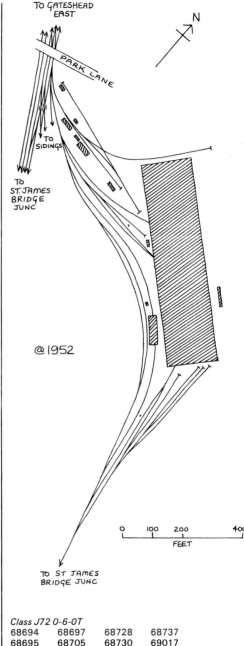

TO GATESHEAD EAST

PARK LANE

N

TO SIDINGS

TO ST. JAMES BRIDGE JUNC

@1952

TO ST JAMES BRIDGE JUNC

0   100   200   400
FEET

Class J72 0-6-0T
68694   68697   68728   68737
68695   68705   68730   69017

Total 44

The shed at Borough Gardens was a roundhouse accommodating four turntables in a line formation

105

The interior of Borough Gardens shed in 1957.
P. J. Kelley

and was situated half a mile south-east of Gateshead East station. It was sometimes referred to as 'Park Lane' because of its close proximity to the Junction of that name.

The shed was re-coded 52J in September 1958 and closed in June the following year. The engines were re-allocated as follows: 18 to Gateshead 52A, 12 to Blaydon 52C, three to Tyne Dock 52H, two each to West Hartlepool 51C, South Blyth 52F, Consett 52K and one each to York 50A, Thornaby 51L, North Blyth 52F and Sunderland 52G (total 43).

Apart from the shunting advantage, roundhouse depots afforded much more space between locos as will be seen here in this 1956 view of Borough Gardens interior. A. E. Ellis

Class Q6 0-8-0 No 63346 (52J) outside Borough
Gardens in 1959. N. Skinner

The northern-most entrance to Borough Gardens
shed in the mid-1950s amid the usual ash and
clinker problem. B. Hilton Collection

A broadside view of 'J72' 0-6-0T No 69017 (54C)
inside Borough Gardens in 1950. H. C. Casserley

54D CONSETT

Pre-Grouping Origin: NER
Gazetteer Ref: 27 C4
Closed: 1965
Shed-Codes: 54D (1949-1958)
52K (1958-1965)
Allocations: 1950 (54D)

Class Q6 0-8-0

63346	63361	63404	63439
63357	63365	63418	63455
63359	63372	63433	

Class N8 0-6-2T

69394	69395

Total 13

Allocations: 1959 (52K)

Class Q6 0-8-0

63345	63365	63404	63427	63455
63357	63372	63406	63433	
63359	63379	63418	63439	

Class J94 0-6-0ST
68019

Total 14

Allocations: 1965 (52K)

Class K1 2-6-0
62027

Class Q6 0-8-0

63357	63379	63395	63455
63368	63394	63427	

Total 8

Previously a single lane establishment, Consett shed was doubled in size about 1950 with the provision of a parallel structure.

The motive power reorganisation of September 1958 resulted in Consett being re-coded 52K.

The shed closed in May 1965 and the remaining seven locos were dispersed as follows: Nos 63368/94 to West Hartlepool 51C, Nos 62027/63427 to North Blyth 52F, Nos 63379/455 to Tyne Dock 52H and No 63395 to Sunderland 52G.

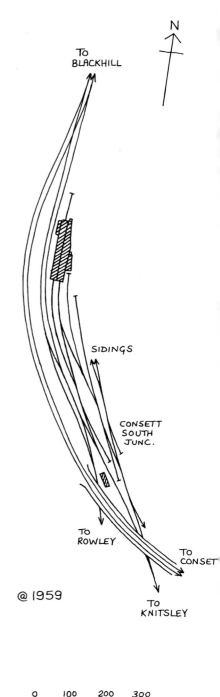

N

To
BLACKHILL

SIDINGS

CONSETT
SOUTH
JUNC.

To
ROWLEY

To
CONSET

@ 1959

To
KNITSLEY

0	100	200	300

FEET

One of Consett's longer serving 'Q6' 0-8-0s,
No 63357, rests at is home depot in 1963.
A. G. Ellis

A powerful Class Q7 0-8-0 No 63460 (52H) heads a
RCTS and SLS joint 'special' (NER tour 1963) past
Consett shed in September 1963.   N. Skinner

Looking south-east across the yard at Consett in
1959 clearly showing the limited stabling space.
K. Fairey

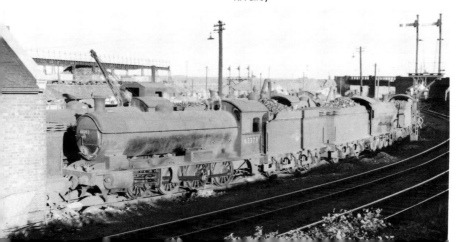

Consett shed in 1954 portraying the recently constructed westerly section on the left. Class WD 2-8-0 No 90045 (54D) can just be seen through the entrance of the original right-hand building.
Photomatic

55A LEEDS HOLBECK
55B STOURTON

Refer to 20A Leeds Holbeck, 20B Stourton within the LMR volume. Both depots were of Midland Railway origin and did not transfer to the North Eastern Region until 1957.

55C FARNLEY JUNCTION

Refer to 25G Farnley Junction within the LMR volume. The shed was of LNWR origin and did not transfer to the North Eastern Region until 1956.

55D ROYSTON
55E NORMANTON

Refer to 20C Royston, 20D Normanton within the LMR volume. The depots were of LMS (1932) and LYR origins respectively and did not transfer to the North Eastern Region until 1957.

55F BRADFORD MANNINGHAM

Refer to 20E Bradford Manningham within the LMR volume. The shed was of Midland Railway origin and did not transfer to the North Eastern until 1957.

55G HUDDERSFIELD

Refer to 25B Huddersfield within the LMR volume. The depot was of LNWR origin and did not transfer to the North Eastern Region until 1957.

55H LEEDS NEVILLE HILL

See 50B Leeds Neville Hill in this volume.

56A WAKEFIELD

Refer to 25A Wakefield within the LMR volume. The shed was of LYR origin and did not transfer to the North Eastern Region until 1956.

56B ARDSLEY
56C COPLEY HILL

Refer to 37A Ardsley, 37B Copley Hill within the ER volume. Both depots were of GNR origin and did not transfer to the North Eastern Region until 1956.

56D MIRFIELD
56E SOWERBY BRIDGE
56F LOW MOOR

Refer to 25D Mirfield, 25E Sowerby Bridge, 25F Low Moor within the LMR volume. All three depots were of LYR origin and did not transfer to the North Eastern Region until 1956.

56G BRADFORD HAMMERTON STREET

Refer to 37C Bradford Hammerton Street within the ER volume. The shed was of GNR origin and did not transfer to the North Eastern Region until 1956.

List of Shed-Codes

The following list sets out every shed-code that existed for steam Motive Power Depots under the North Eastern Region from 1949 to 1967 along with each venue and its length of occupancy.

50A	York 1949-67
50B	Leeds Neville Hill 1949-60
	Hull Dairycoates 1960-67
50C	Selby 1949-59
50D	Starbeck 1949-59
	Goole 1960-67
50E	Scarborough 1949-63
50F	Malton 1949-63
50G	Whitby 1949-59
51A	Darlington 1949-66
51B	Newport 1949-58
51C	West Hartlepool 1949-67
51D	Middlesbrough 1949-58
51E	Stockton 1949-59
51F	West Auckland 1949-64
51G	Haverton Hill 1949-59
51H	Kirkby Stephen 1949-58
51J	Northallerton 1949-63
51K	Saltburn 1949-58
51L	Thornaby 1958-64
52A	Gateshead 1949-65
52B	Heaton 1949-63
52C	Blaydon 1949-63
52D	Tweedmouth 1949-66
52E	Percy Main 1949-65

52F	North & South Blyth 1949-67
52G	Sunderland 1958-67
52H	Tyne Dock 1958-67
52J	Borough Gardens 1958-59
52K	Consett 1958-65
53A	Hull Dairycoates 1949-60
53B	Hull Botanic Gardens 1949-59
53C	Hull Springhead 1949-58
53D	Bridlington 1949-58
53E	Cudworth 1949-51
	Goole 1956-60
54A	Sunderland 1949-58
54B	Tyne Dock 1949-58
54C	Borough Gardens 1949-58
54D	Consett 1949-58
55A	Leeds Holbeck 1957-67
55B	Stourton 1957-67
55C	Farnley Junction 1956-66
55D	Royston 1957-67
55E	Normanton 1957-67
55F	Bradford Manningham 1957-67
55G	Huddersfield 1957-67
55H	Leeds Neville Hill 1960-66
56A	Wakefield 1956-67
56B	Ardsley 1956-65
56C	Copley Hill 1956-64
56D	Mirfield 1956-67
56E	Sowerby Bridge 1956-64
56F	Low Moor 1956-67
56G	Bradford Hammerton Street 1956-58

Index